Trump's Turn

Winning the New Civil War

Ed Brodow

Trump's Turn:
Winning the New Civil War

Published by Tout Droit Publishing
Cover Design by Don Zirlilight

Books by Ed Brodow

Tyranny of the Minority
In Lies We Trust
Negotiation Boot Camp
Beating the Success Trap
Fixer
Women From Venus
Negotiate with Confidence

Contents

Introduction: The Baby and the Bathwater

"If you have always believed that everyone should play by the same rules and be judged by the same standards, that would have gotten you labeled a radical 60 years ago, a liberal 30 years ago and a racist today."

Thomas Sowell

For most of my life, I was not a political person. I grew up as a Democrat because my family and most of my Brooklyn neighbors were Democrats. As a former Marine, I always took the privilege of voting seriously but never spent a lot of time worrying about politics. All of that changed dramatically during the presidential election campaign of 2008. When a group of my liberal friends discovered that I was not voting for their hero, Barack Obama, they joined forces to call me a racist. They didn't care what my reasons were—and I had some good ones—for them I was a racist, pure and simple.

Thanks to my former friends, the new direction of the political Left was revealed to me in all its dystopian glory. I realized that the Democratic Party of today is not the party of my parents and grandparents. The great irony is that the liberal Democrat of my youth is today's conservative Republican. The Democrats of today want to "throw out the baby with the bathwater." Linguistic scholars have traced this popular idiomatic expression to a German proverb that is more than 500 years old. According to *Wikipedia*, it refers to "an avoidable error in which something good is eliminated when trying to get rid of something bad, or in other words, rejecting the favorable along with the unfavorable." Throwing out the baby with the bathwater can be taken as a metaphor for a spectacular flaw in leftist ideology.

The extremists that are taking over the Democratic Party hope to fulfill Barack Obama's pledge to "fundamentally

1

transform America." Obama hates this country. His objective as president was not merely to change the US—*to throw out the bathwater*—but to completely eradicate American values—*the baby*. Obama's ideological heirs believe that the US is a racist society run by a cabal of immoral white people. To correct this perceived abuse, they want the destruction of all existing political, economic, and social institutions. In the process, they intend to obliterate the values that make ours a truly extraordinary country:

- Respect for the rights of the individual
- Free speech (over political correctness)
- Meritocracy (over affirmative action and identity politics)
- Due process and the rule of law
- Equality of opportunity via free market competition (as opposed to equality of outcome via socialism)
- The acceptance of personal responsibility

The conflict over value systems has escalated into a new civil war. It is not a war of armies and weapons, nor is it simply Trump versus the Deep State. It is a war of visions. Liberals and conservatives each have a different vision for the future of the nation. Conservatives believe in the Constitution and the rule of law. The vision of progressive liberals, Obama's vision, is an authoritarian socialist nation run by unaccountable bureaucrats—an approximation of Venezuela, somewhere between Stalin's Soviet Union and Orwell's *1984*. For that reason alone, we are fortunate that Donald Trump is our president instead of Hillary Clinton, Bernie Sanders, Elizabeth Warren, or one of the other "democratic socialists." Obama had eight years to project his neo-Marxist will on the United States. Now it is Trump's turn.

While change as a general proposition is desirable and inevitable, it ought not to be accomplished at the expense of everything that is good about the status quo. Leftists have tried extreme versions of change in Soviet Russia, Maoist China, Cuba, and Venezuela—in every instance it blew up in their faces. A much better model can be found in English history, where the most significant changes occurred via evolution rather than revolution.

The United States was built on the English model. Our Founding Fathers abandoned King George and a few of the arbitrary laws of the eighteenth century but retained many of the laudable aspects of British governance. When the rebellious colonials threw out the bathwater, they had the good sense to keep the baby. It would be tragic if we were to forget the example they set for us.

History will record the period between 2016-19 as a key transition in American politics. The victory of Donald J. Trump represents a critical rejection by the American people of a great deal of dirty bathwater: Obama's anti-American agenda, the socialist ideology of the new Left, and the self-serving political class that populates Washington, DC. Even though Trump won the election and was vindicated by the Mueller Report, many of my conservative friends are afraid to go public with their political preferences for fear that they will be assaulted by disciples of Obama, Hillary, Alexandria Ocasio-Cortez, and Maxine Waters. It is essential for conservatives to speak up in the face of leftist violence and intimidation.

The essays in this volume expound on the issues and people that played a significant role in the 2016 presidential election and its stormy aftermath. They appeared in *American Thinker, Townhall, Daily Caller, LifeZette, Media Equalizer, Newsmax* and other conservative on-line news magazines. I am grateful to the

Internet for providing alternatives to the Democratic-owned mainstream media.

My essays attempt to make some sense out of the conflict between conservatives and liberals, between capitalists and "democratic socialists," and between Trump supporters and Never Trumpers. Topics include the reasons behind the Trump revolution, leftist ideology, immigration policy, political correctness, climate change, globalism, diversity, identity politics, Islamic terrorism, and sexual politics. The topics were chosen based on what people are thinking and wondering about and arguing over.

My urge to sit down and write about political events was stimulated whenever something occurred that caused my blood to boil. Such occurrences were frequent. The objective of this volume is to endorse a conservative vision for our country, to encourage the use of evidence and common sense, and to promote critical thinking, which, as always, is in short supply.

Ed Brodow
Monterey, Calif.

Part One: People

"As the US found out in the 1950s, it is depressingly easy to get people who are born into a country that is governed by a Constitution with all the rights and privileges of a free society to give up or devalue it or to panic and abandon the values of that Constitution."

Christopher Hitchens

Chapter 1: Trump and the 2016 Election

Victimhood in the Post-Election Landscape

An angry young woman, participating in a violent street demonstration opposed to the election of Donald J. Trump, informs a TV reporter that she will not allow Trump to take away her rights. On *Facebook*, another angry woman writes: "We need to roll up our sleeves and be ready to remind [Trump] that we aren't going to sit back and surrender to his will. That we are strong and loud and our rights matter."

What rights, exactly, are they afraid of losing? The answer came today in an opinion piece from the *San Francisco Chronicle*. After alleging that Trump wants to "break up our homes," "assault us," "wall out our families," and "ban us from entering the country," the author fires her thunderbolt: Trump will "subject us to unspecified forces of law and order."

The author thinks the imposition of law and order will destroy the rights we enjoy as citizens. She believes that breaking a law you dislike is a right—especially breaking the law by entering the country illegally. Many in the USA, particularly those of college age, have been indoctrinated to believe that the Constitution accords them the right to be "safe" from contradictory political viewpoints and laws they don't like. If you disagree with them, you are taking away their rights. *You are victimizing them.*

Behind all the anti-Trump demonstrations is the desire of the protestors to be perceived as victims. Victims of the system. Victims of racism and sexism. Victims of anything at all just so long as they are entitled to be compensated for their victimhood. So what does it really mean to be a victim? A victim is a person who has come to feel helpless and passive in the face of misfortune or ill treatment. The operative word is "passive," which implies that you do not have to be responsible for your own behavior. You can trash the streets in protest, set fire to cars and property, attack innocent bystanders—with no fear of reprisal. You are not responsible. It is all Trump's fault. He is responsible.

The victimhood argument fails because everyone is responsible for his actions. Being a victim is a choice. No one is a victim unless he chooses to be. What distinguishes humans from "animals" is the ability to choose, to make decisions. When faced with an obstacle, we are challenged with the decision either to (a) overcome the obstacle, or (b) become a victim. When you choose to overcome the obstacle, you are accepting personal responsibility for your life. If you choose to be a victim, your choice implies that someone else has control over your life. "It's not my fault, it's the fault of..." I call this the *victim mentality*: unwillingness to take responsibility for one's own behavior and instead blaming others for life's problems. Victimization has become an industry in the USA.

For this reason, it is not surprising that the post-election landscape is littered with victims strutting their stuff. We have thousands of mostly young people marching down the streets and boulevards of our cities with a big chip on their collective shoulder. The person they wanted to be president lost the election. Their teachers told them they have a right to feel safe and now they feel unsafe.

Because these people are victims, they have the right to deny others their rights. They have the right to tell you who to vote for. They have the right to disregard law and order at their pleasure. They have the right to free education, free healthcare, free living subsidies. They have the right to enter the country illegally and receive unearned benefits. There is only one problem. Everything has a cost, and the cost of denying the rule of law is chaos and anarchy.

So let's make a choice. Do we have a real country or do we have anarchy? As Bill O'Reilly has observed, the protestors are encouraged by a permissive, progressive society. The violent protestors are not victims. These people have made a choice and must be held to account. They are criminals and should be punished severely.

Daily Surge, November 14, 2016

The Mythic Significance of Donald Trump

When I was a little boy, I was mesmerized by Bing Crosby's rendition of Irving Berlin's *White Christmas*.

> *"I'm dreaming of a white Christmas*
> *Just like the ones I used to know*
> *Where the treetops glisten and children listen*
> *To hear sleigh bells in the snow."*

It was, and still is, one of my favorite songs. Then there was the 1942 *Holiday Inn* movie, featuring Bing singing the song in an idyllic resort setting complete with gently falling snow and a roaring fireside. I recall watching it on TV. My child's imagination interpreted this image of warmth as a promise that the future would be a safe, comfortable, emotionally supportive place.

The holiday represented by Christmas is a classic myth of home and hearth. It is the contemporary version of the winter solstice that human beings have celebrated for millennia. Even today, when I hear Bing crooning those lyrics, something wonderful happens to my body as I am transported back in time to that early recollection.

Then a truly horrific awakening occurs. I recognize that life is not like that at all. They lied to us—the world we live in is anything but safe, either physically or emotionally. But, despite the lie, the myth of *White Christmas* always gives me hope. According to mythology guru Joseph Campbell, myths have helped human beings to survive the many challenges of life. *White Christmas* provided a beacon to guide me through what Campbell referred to as the "dark forest." No matter how bleak the future seemed, my psyche could always fall back on the beautiful promise of *White Christmas*.

With the leftist notion of political correctness, the myth of *White Christmas* has taken a hit to the solar plexus. It contains a double whammy: *white* and *Christmas*. PC has managed to destroy *Christmas* by telling us that it represents our degenerate, racist society. And the mere use of the simple word *white* causes progressives to throw up. For these people, *white* can't possibly refer to the calming effect of falling snow. Instead, any mention of *white* must be a reflection of the supremacist society in which *people of color* are oppressed. That sublime image of the world that I've been toting around since childhood has been transformed into North Korea.

Barack Obama deserves much of the credit for the decline of American mythology. During the eight years of the Obama administration, we were supposed to feel guilty about being American. From the first day of his presidency, Obama was apologizing all over the world for what he perceived as America's shortcomings and transgressions. "Never before in American history have we had a president who seeks decline," wrote Dinesh D'Souza in *Obama's America: Unmaking the American Dream*, "who is actually attempting to downsize his country." When Obama said, "If you've got a business, you didn't build that. Somebody else made that happen," he invalidated the American Dream. A similar assault on the image of *White Christmas* would not be far behind.

The same trend is afflicting Europe, says Douglas Murray in *The Strange Death of Europe*. Murray suggests that Europe is surrendering to Islam because Europeans no longer believe their culture is worth preserving. They have been convinced by their politicians that European culture is flawed and evil. The myths that sustained the cultural heritage of Europe have been replaced by the welfare state. Europeans have traded their freedom for government handouts. "If enough people in a society are suffering from a form of exhaustion," Murray writes, "might it not be that the society they are living in has become exhausted?"

Enter Donald Trump. He has given America a new lease on life. On a mythic level, he has re-energized America by reaffirming its intrinsic values. He wants to "make America great again." Why should anyone feel guilty about being part of the greatest social experiment in human history? We have a right to feel proud of our accomplishments. It is thanks to Trump that *White Christmas*, the American Dream, and other positive images about our country have been revived. We need supportive myths so we can move into the future with optimism rather than despair. The success of our country depends upon it.

Lantern of Liberty, June 19, 2018

Donald Trump: Crazy as a Fox

Ever since November 8, an avalanche of accusations has been leveled by the Left against President Trump. Liberal mouthpieces and the mainstream media, angry as hell because their candidate lost, say that Trump is racist, bigoted, sexist, misogynistic, anti-Semitic, Islamophobic, and who knows what else. All these allegations are based on circumstantial evidence or someone's opinion. None of the allegations bears any resemblance to the truth. All of the allegations appear to be driven by political ideology. One of the most disgraceful accusations is that Trump is the second coming of Adolf Hitler. When it originates with Rachel Maddow, Chris Matthews, or Paul Krugman, the accusation is easy to disregard. But now we have a new accuser who seems to have better credentials.

During a conference held at the Yale School of Medicine, psychotherapist Dr. John Gartner, formerly of Johns Hopkins University, said Trump is unfit to be president because of "dangerous mental illness." Citing paranoia together with delusional and grandiose thinking, Gartner told fellow psychologists that they have an ethical duty to warn the public about Trump's dangerous condition. On Jesse Watters' Fox TV show, Gartner specifically compared Trump's "malignant narcissism" to Hitler's.

In a similar vein, New York University psychiatrist Dr. James Gilligan compared Trump with murderers and rapists. Gilligan claims he can recognize these people "a mile away," and Trump is definitely one of them.

This entire line of attack is bogus for three reasons: (1) none of the accusers has analyzed Trump in the flesh; (2) other psychological professionals disagree; and (3) the attack is contradicted by the facts.

The statements against Trump violate the "Goldwater Rule," part of the American Psychiatric Association's code of ethics, which prohibits members from giving a professional opinion about a public figure they have not examined personally. Gartner doesn't think that makes sense. He believes that opinions of others have more relevance than a personal psychiatric interview. In other words, he prefers to rely on hearsay and speculation. Yale University, wisely covering its behind, has attempted to distance itself from Gartner's accusations: "The opinions presented at the conference did not represent those of the Department of Psychology or Yale University."

The contrary viewpoint is expressed by Dr. Keith Ablow, a noted psychiatrist and Fox News contributor. Pointing to Trump's phenomenal success both professionally and personally, Ablow argues that, "Donald Trump is stone cold sane. Those who assert otherwise are political opportunists, or fools, or both." Trump has many idiosyncrasies, notes Ablow, but they will all work to his advantage as president. Many geniuses are idiosyncratic, he says, and "we've got a genius in the oval office." Ablow reminds us that Abraham Lincoln, Winston Churchill, and Mahatma Gandhi reportedly suffered from major depression or bipolar disorder. "Psychiatric illness," Ablow says, "does not, a priori, disqualify a person from rendering extraordinary service to mankind."

Renowned psychiatrist Dr. Allen Frances, who wrote the criteria defining "narcissistic personality disorder," sent a letter to the *New York Times* in which he says that Trump "may be a world-class narcissist, but this doesn't make him mentally ill because he does not suffer from the stress and impairment required to diagnose mental disorder."

Independent Journal Review reported the story of Inga Andrews, who grew up in Dusseldorf, Germany during Hitler's reign. "Trump is not like Hitler," she says. "Just because a leader wants order doesn't mean they're a dictator." Comparing Trump to Hitler is pure propaganda, Andrews says. "All you have to do is read some books about that period to see how wrong that theory is." Andrews may not be a psychiatrist, but her life experience lends credence to her viewpoint.

I would like to add my own reaction to the "Trump is crazy" accusations. First, I cannot help but think that many of the accusers are Democrats who attack Trump in support of their own left-wing political agenda. But there is another factor that should be taken into consideration. Psychiatry is arguably the least objective of all "scientific" fields. "The subjective nature of the psychiatric diagnosis has always been a problem," according to *New Statesman*. The diagnosis of mental disorder is not the same as a legitimate medical diagnosis of a disease. Mental illness is determined by psychiatrists literally voting on what is and what is not a mental disorder. This is a political, not medical, process.

"'Mental illness' is terribly misleading," says Dr. Allen Frances, "because the 'mental disorders' we diagnose are no more than descriptions of what clinicians observe people do or say." Given the very nature of psychiatry, there will always be a difference of interpretation among practitioners. Jesse Watters did an admirable job of suggesting that Gartner might be the one who is paranoid. At the very least, the advice of Dr. Gartner and his friends ought to be taken with a healthy dose of skepticism.

Daily Surge, May 9, 2017

Nazi Comparison: The Shoe is on the Wrong Foot

Everywhere I look lately, Trump is being compared to Hitler. For example, two photos were just posted on *Facebook*. One was Hitler saying that Jews are animals; the second was Trump saying that Mexicans are animals. The message is that Trump is another Hitler. Of course, Trump never made either of those statements. He said that violent MS-13 gang members are animals. "The quotation attributed to President Trump," said *Snopes.com*, "was both inaccurate and left out the full context behind his remarks, which referred to undocumented and deported migrants convicted of crimes." The mainstream media, unfortunately, is all too willing to report Trump's words incorrectly.

The woman who posted the photos on *Facebook* is a classic example of an educated professional caught up in Trump Derangement Syndrome. She is pushing a false, vulgar argument because it supports her political view. Where did she get the idea? Did she invent it? Instead of thinking for herself, she is regurgitating the propaganda she picked up from fake news media. Here are some of the sources she may have borrowed from:

   • *New York Magazine*: "Like Hitler, Trump is a radical, authoritarian figure."

   • *MSNBC*/Joe Scarborough: "You can be offended if you want, but that's out of Hitler's playbook."

   • *MSNBC*/Chris Matthews: Trump's inaugural speech was "Hitlerian."

   • *Time Magazine*: "The comparison between Hitler and Trump is so poignant."

- *CNN*: "Barack Obama was right" to compare the rise of Donald Trump to the rise of Adolf Hitler.

- *The Forward*: "Yes, you should be comparing Trump to Hitler."

Now that the trend has been established, let me get to the point. If we are going to compare an element of our country to Nazi Germany, it really ought to be the *Deep State*—the unaccountable bureaucrats who are running the show in Washington. Under Obama, the powers of the federal government were weaponized against political opponents on the Right. This police state strategy has been executed by the Deep State and supported by a press that is owned by the Democratic Party. This is what the Nazis and the Soviets did. Now it is happening here.

When I refer to the Deep State, I am using Newt Gingrich's definition: "A permanent state of massive bureaucracies that do whatever they want." The Deep State is the huge unelected bureaucracy that represents the "big" in our big government. From a nation in which corrupt politicians once ruled with an iron fist, we have progressed to one in which politicians have surrendered control to an administrative class that makes the major decisions with little accountability or direction from anyone. They mostly live in the Washington, DC, area and contribute heavily to the Democratic Party, whose values they espouse. Your vote means nothing when the people you elect to serve in Congress are not the ones who make the rules. The result is that our country is looking more and more like North Korea.

In a totalitarian state, justice has a double standard—one for the party in power and another for the opposition. Thanks to the Deep State, the double standard of justice in America looks like this: the deliberate targeting of conservative organizations by the IRS while liberal groups get a free pass; the prosecution by the

Justice Department of conservative political opponents, e.g., Paul Manafort, Dinesh D'Souza, and General Michael Flynn, while "progressive" felons are let off the hook, e.g., Hillary Clinton, James Comey, Eric Holder, and Loretta Lynch; and the ongoing effort by Justice Department and FBI bureaucrats to invalidate a legitimate presidential election.

Evidence is mounting that the FBI under James Comey knowingly and willfully protected Hillary Clinton from a mountain of potential felony prosecutions, and the Mueller investigation is part of a thinly veiled attempt by the Deep State to destroy the Trump presidency. We are witnessing the rise of the Nazi-like leftist group Antifa. A leftist mob surrounded the home of Homeland Security Secretary Kirstjen Nielsen. The most frightening example of totalitarian abuse was the middle-of-the-night assault by gun-toting FBI agents against the Virginia home of Trump supporter Paul Manafort. When I heard about this, the image of Gestapo tactics immediately came to mind. If the FBI can scare Manafort and his wife out of their pajamas, they can do it to you and to me.

Let the record show that Donald Trump's values are the opposite of fascist ones, while the Democratic Party embraces the totalitarian aim of bigger government at the expense of individual liberties, especially freedom of speech. The "swamp" that Trump has sworn to drain is composed of the entrenched political hacks of the Deep State. They are terrified by the prospect of a political outsider who wants to wipe them out. Their defense is comparing Trump to Hitler, a dishonest form of psychological projection. If our country is threatened by Nazi-like forces, let's get real. They are coming not from the Right but from the Left.

Liberty Unyielding, June 27, 2018

Why No Outcry Against Failed DoJ Coup D'Etat?

We are witnessing another tragic event in the saga of Donald Trump's presidency. Andrew McCabe, former acting director of the FBI, admitted that the Department of Justice attempted to remove the duly-elected President of the United States from office with no evidence of wrongdoing. Yet where is the outcry? The moral outrage? The demand for justice? I didn't hear it. Did you? That is unacceptable.

Instead of setting off a chorus of demands for an immediate investigation, Mr. McCabe became a media celebrity as he appeared on CBS's *60 Minutes* to plug his new book, ironically titled, *The Threat: How the FBI Protects America in the Age of Terror and Trump*. The book alleges that, "Right now the greatest threat to the United States comes from within, as President Trump and his administration ignore the law ... and undermine the U.S. Constitution." McCabe was one of the top echelon in the FBI and DoJ that wanted desperately to prevent Donald Trump from sitting in the Oval Office.

Segue to this week's interview on *60 Minutes*. McCabe said he ordered an obstruction of justice probe against the president after Trump fired FBI Director James Comey. Then he claimed that former Acting Attorney General Rod Rosenstein raised the issue of actually removing the president from office. Scott Pelley, who conducted the interview, describes McCabe's confession:

> *"There were meetings at the Justice Department at which it was discussed whether the vice president and a majority of the Cabinet could be brought together to remove the president of the United States under the 25th Amendment. They were counting noses... They were speculating, 'This person would be with us. That*

person would not be.' They were counting noses in that effort."

McCabe detailed his co-conspirators' roles in the planned and implemented coup against Trump. Using a fake Russian dossier as a pretext, Rosenstein appointed former FBI Director Robert Mueller to investigate Trump with the intention of bringing down his presidency. The failure of the plot does not diminish its nefarious intent.

"Any Justice Department official who even mentioned the 25th amendment in the context of President Trump," said retired Harvard Law Professor Alan Dershowitz, "has committed a grievous offense against the Constitution." If McCabe's comments are true, Dershowitz added, "it is clearly an attempt at a coup d'etat."

Reacting to the *60 Minutes* revelations, President Trump blasted McCabe as a "disgrace" to the FBI and to the country. "Andrew McCabe is a national disgrace," agreed Michael Goodwin in the *New York Post.* "He was part of the most corrupt and most partisan leadership team in FBI history and … has reminded us once again that there really is a powerful deep state, and that there has not been a full accounting of rampant FBI misconduct during the presidential campaign of 2016."

Although the Mueller investigation has the taint of illegality—appointment of a special counsel must be based on the commission of a crime—no one in the government has attempted to stop it. Although federal law prohibits any attempt to advocate or encourage the overthrow of the government, there has been no attempt to prosecute McCabe and his fellow conspirators. The politicized DoJ has committed offenses that we would normally associate with third-world dictatorships. When the police arm of the government goes after political opponents, we are sliding down the road to Stalinism. And still McCabe's revelations, in point of fact, have been received with little more than apathy.

"There is also still too much we don't know," Goodwin laments, "about the role top aides to then-President Barack Obama and higher-ups in the Justice Department played in spying on the Trump campaign and leaks of classified information for partisan purposes. In short, what is arguably the greatest scandal in the history of America remains mostly hidden from the public."

We are wasting a chance to bring the scandal out into the open. So I repeat: An attempt was made to bring down the president. *Where is the outcry? The moral outrage? The demand for justice?* Something very profound has faded from the public forum and we are not better off for its disappearance. What we are missing is the desire to achieve a proactive resolution for scandals like this one. The newly-confirmed attorney general, William Barr, has an opportunity to take action. Will he do it, or will he emulate his predecessor by sweeping it under the rug? We are about to find out.

Clash Daily, February 18, 2019

When Facts Get In the Way—Blame Trump

The most significant take-away from my college education was learning to rely on evidence over opinion, hearsay, and rumor. "Everyone is entitled to his own opinion," said Daniel Patrick Moynihan, "but not his own facts." Never in a million years did I suspect that political correctness would come along and overrule Senator Moynihan's famous dictum. That's right—the geniuses of the Democratic Party Brain Trust are attempting to create their own facts.

We have a clear statement of two pertinent facts from the Mueller Report: (1) There was no Trump-Russia collusion; and (2) There is no basis for a charge of obstruction against the president. This comes after 2,800 subpoenas, 500 search warrants, and 500 witnesses over two years of investigation. Thanks to the mainstream media's penchant for fake news, Mueller's conclusion was the opposite of what the Democrats were anticipating. Trump was correct when he tweeted, "No Collusion, No Obstruction, Complete and Total EXONERATION."

Yet every time I turn on CNN or MSNBC, the insanity hits me right in the face. House Judiciary Committee Chair Jerrold Nadler, interviewed by Chris Wallace after Mueller's finding of no collusion, had the gall to insist, "We know there was collusion." What is this refusal to accept the conclusion of the special counsel if not Nadler's attempt to create his own facts? Similarly, Democratic presidential candidate "Beto" O'Rourke tweeted, "You have a president, who in my opinion, beyond the shadow of a doubt, sought to collude with the Russian government."

House Intelligence Committee Chairman Adam Schiff, speaking on ABC's *This Week*, insisted there is "ample evidence of collusion in plain sight." In fact, he added, "Every act that I've pointed to as evidence of collusion has now been borne out by the [Mueller] report." Did Schiff forget to take his meds? Chris Wallace reminded Schiff on *Fox News Sunday* that special counsel Robert Mueller failed to find "the kind of coordination" that Schiff claims took place. Schiff tried to sidestep Wallace's rebuke by using classic doubletalk: "The fact that you may not be able to prove beyond a reasonable doubt a criminal conspiracy doesn't mean there is an absence of evidence of crime." Schiff is ignoring the basis of our legal system that if you can't prove a crime beyond a reasonable doubt, there is no crime.

Senator Elizabeth Warren, another deluded member of Congress, continues to insist that the Mueller Report justifies impeaching the president. "We cannot be an America that says it is OK for a president of the United States to try and block an investigation into a foreign attack on our country or an investigation into that president's own misbehavior—so I have called on the House to initiate impeachment proceedings." What the hell is Pocahontas raving about? Trump did nothing to impede Mueller's investigation and actually cooperated on a massive scale. "Some things are bigger than politics," Warren argued. Yes senator, how about "some things" such as FACTS?

Actor Robert DeNiro, an unofficial member of the Democratic Brain Trust, also contradicted the special counsel's report. "Trump obstructed justice all the time," said the star of *Raging Bull*. "I mean, what are we talking about? It's right before our eyes." The man may be a fine actor but he obviously needs glasses. DeNiro warned that if the Mueller report doesn't eventually give leftists what they want, "There's going to be a lot of mass demonstrations, a lot of protests." What DeNiro is saying is, *"If the facts don't support my position, the hell with the facts."* This could be the rallying cry of today's progressive liberal Democrat. As he advocates for diversity out of one side of his mouth, the progressive rails against viewpoint diversity—also known as free speech—out of the other. "Diversity" means "it is great to look different as long as you think the way I do." Whatever you say that contradicts leftist ideology is "hate speech." The Democrats are using this warped thinking to justify their assault on the facts. If a fact denies the validity of a Democratic talking point, that fact constitutes hate speech and must be relegated to the trash bin.

This is the beginning of totalitarianism. "For, after all," wrote George Orwell in *1984*, "how do we know that two and two make four? Or that the force of gravity works? Or that the past is unchangeable? If both the past and the external world exist only in the mind, and if the mind itself is controllable—what then?" And let's not forget Joseph Goebbels: "The truth is the mortal enemy of the lie, and thus by extension, the truth is the greatest enemy of the state."

Townhall, April 22, 2019

Chapter 2: Obama

Hope-a-Dope: Obama's Deception

Boxer Muhammad Ali had a strategy called "rope-a-dope" where he would dupe his opponent. By pretending to be trapped against the ropes, Ali would tire out the other fighter and then come back to win the bout. Barack Obama has used the concept of hope in a similar way in order to dupe the American public. I call it "hope-a-dope." Obama won the presidency with his brilliant campaign slogan, "Hope and Change"—brilliant not because of what it meant, but rather because of what it did not mean. All by itself, "Hope and Change" doesn't mean a damn thing. Obama's slogan was pure nonsense on purpose.

"Hope and Change" was intended to seduce gullible voters who were fed up after George W. Bush's second term in office. Hope and change. Change and hope. You can go along with it but you can't attack it because there is no "it." What would you say? "I am against hope and against change!" You would wake up in Bellevue wearing a straitjacket. Everyone wants hope and change. For millions of voters, it did not matter what Obama meant by hope. They voted for him because of what *they* thought it meant, not because of what *he* thought it meant.

Enter Donald Trump. Trump's election is a rejection of Obama's concept of hope, which reflects his desire to minimalize all things American. Trump stands for the hopes and dreams of all those who were left out by Obama's anti-American platform. In an attempt to spin this around, Michelle Obama says that Trump's election is the destruction of hope. "See, now, we are feeling what not having hope feels like," Mrs. Obama told Oprah

Winfrey last week. "Hope is necessary. It's a necessary concept and Barack didn't just talk about hope because he thought it was just a nice slogan to get votes." Who do you think you're kidding, Michelle? That is exactly why he talked about it.

"He and I and so many," Mrs. Obama continued, "believe that—what else do you have if you don't have hope? What do you give your kids if you can't give them hope?" She is clearly suggesting that only the Obamas' definition of hope is correct, thereby invalidating the hopes and aspirations of the millions who voted for Trump. In reality, Mrs. Obama is nothing more than a sore loser. If you don't believe in what we want you to believe, she is saying, you are an enemy of hope. Wow! That is monumental arrogance and, frankly, it offends me.

Yes, Barack Obama got away with it for eight years, but now his hope-a-dope strategy has been unmasked. Now we know what Obama intended by his version of hope and change. The change he tried to induce was the destruction of American exceptionalism by reducing her influence on the world stage and by bringing her down economically and militarily. Obama hoped that the United States would become Denmark. An unexceptional nation, divided from within, and weighed down by the insatiable demands of a massive nanny state. No thank you, Mr. Obama. Please take your hope-a-dope somewhere else, anywhere else, but not here.

Michelle Obama sees the end of hope. For all our sakes, I hope she is correct—I hope we have seen the last of the Obamas' version of hope. I'm tired of being duped by hope-a-dope.

Daily Surge, December 21, 2016

The Hypocrite-in-Chief Rides Again

Former President Obama has criticized President Trump's temporary immigration ban on citizens from seven Middle East countries. Here is Obama's statement urging people to resist:

> *"Citizens exercising their Constitutional right to assemble, organize and have their voices heard by their elected officials is exactly what we expect to see when American values are at stake."*

Obama encourages anti-Trump protests on the grounds that the immigration ban violates American values. This critique is uniquely hypocritical. For eight years, I watched Obama's concentrated assault on our values. How can he pretend to defend these values after doing so much to undo them? "He pledged to 'fundamentally transform America,'" said Joseph Farah, editor of *WorldNetDaily*, "and he has done his level best to destroy it through fanning flames of hatred of all it stands for both inside the country and abroad." *American Thinker* agreed: "Barack Obama is trying to destroy America's essence, that commitment to liberty that makes her unique in this world, and that makes her uniquely American."

Where does Obama stand with respect to American values? "If the desire to knock America off its pedestal, to redistribute American income to other countries, to shrink America's footprint in the world, makes you anti-American," said author and political commentator Dinesh D'Souza, "then Obama is in fact anti-American." Here is a list of American values followed by Obama's negative interpretations:

1. *Success is the reward of hard work* (myth of the self-made man): Obama attempted to destroy this value with his condescending statement, "If you've got a business—

you didn't build that. Somebody else made that happen."
As the *Daily News* pointed out, Obama attacked the
individualism inherent in the American dream.

2. *Freedom of the individual* (The state exists to optimize
individual freedoms, not to control the individual):
"Every single one of [Obama's] initiatives," says
American Thinker, "is directed at increasing government
control in every area, with a corresponding decrease in
individual liberty."

3. *Separation of powers* (among the three branches of
government): Obama has used executive orders to
bypass the other branches and set up an imperial
presidency. "I think [the Constitution] is an imperfect
document," he said, "and I think this is a document that
reflects some deep flaws in American culture."

4. *Self-reliance* (The American ethos believes we are
accountable for our actions): Obama pushed for
increased entitlements—welfare payments,
unemployment benefits, subsidized healthcare—
because he doesn't think we are able to succeed on our
own. Obama's comments in case after case have denied
the principle of personal responsibility, stoked the fires
of racial discord, and added to the racial divide. "Self
reliance remains the American way," says *Forbes
Magazine*, "despite persistent messages that Americans
need a strong helping hand from the state due to
discrimination and life's other disadvantages."

5. *Equality of opportunity via free market competition*:
Obama did whatever he could to move the country from
meritocracy to race-based tests for "fairness."
Suggesting that we should strive for equality of
outcome—instead of equality of *opportunity*—he

supported the argument that the high rate of black incarceration is the result of unequal treatment by the justice system instead of the higher crime rate in the black community.

6. *Respect for private property, material wealth, and upward mobility*: "U.S. institutions permit individuals to amass wealth (and lose it as well)," said *Forbes*, "and to do so in a single generation. Upward mobility keeps the 'American Dream' alive." Obama argued that the way to end poverty is to take wealth away from the rich. His objectives were the redistribution of income and the enforcement of socialism. In keeping with his globalist philosophy, he pushed for redistributing America's wealth to the third world.

7. *Pride in American exceptionalism*: "American exceptionalism," says *Forbes*, "is the notion that the United States occupies a unique position in the world, offering opportunity and hope to others by its unique balance of public and private interests and constitutional ideals of personal and economic freedom." From the first day of his presidency, Obama was apologizing all over the world for what he perceived as America's shortcomings and transgressions. At the core of Obama's message, said the *Heritage Foundation*, was "the concept that the U.S. is a flawed nation that must seek redemption by apologizing for its past 'sins.'"

At a time when our new president needs support, Obama should at the very least keep his mouth shut. "It is rare for former presidents to criticise their successors," observed *The Telegraph* (UK), "and certainly not just a week and a half after they are sworn in." Instead, Obama is encouraging the very kind of civil disobedience that he tried to suppress during his own presidency. The Obama administration "made a habit of using the power of the state to coerce and compel others to accept its cultural attitudes," argues *The Federalist.* "For him, unity means little dissent. In his last State of the Union, for example, Obama laid out a progressive agenda, then implored us to embrace 'American ideals' as if they were the same." Eight years of his hypocrisy are enough.

Daily Surge, February 2, 2017

Mirror, Mirror on the Wall—Obama's the Biggest Liar of Them All!

In the interest of remaining positive, I always like to find something good in people. Even though I don't like Barack Obama, I've been thinking, "What is there about him that is worth remembering?" You'll be happy to know that I came up with something: Obama is without a doubt the biggest liar I have ever seen. He just proved it with his speech at the University of Illinois.

Obama began his speech by accusing the Republicans of fomenting division. "The politics of division and resentment and paranoia," he said, "has unfortunately found a home in the Republican Party." In fact, it is the Democratic Party that has made "divisiveness" into a house guest. The Democrats use their perverted version of "diversity," says author Mark Levin, to exploit discontented elements in American society and to divide people against themselves. Obama's presidency played into this leftist strategy of "divide and conquer." After eight years of Obama, race relations are worse than ever and the country is on the verge of civil war.

Then Obama said that our democracy depends on people voting for Democrats, adding that he wants to restore "honesty and decency" in government. This is pure hypocrisy from a man who has shown contempt for the Constitution, a man who weaponized the powers of the federal government against his political opponents with the IRS targeting conservatives and selective prosecution of people like Dinesh D'Souza. "Obama created a climate in which the potentially criminal misuse of the DOJ and the FBI, as currently being unraveled, was not just acceptable but perhaps encouraged," wrote Monica Crowley in

The Hill, "thereby giving rise to what could be the most dangerous scandal in American history." There is no evidence that Obama's Democratic successors are likely to do any better for the cause of democracy.

In spite of all this, the University of Illinois evidently agrees that Obama is the savior of democracy. They gave him an award for ethics in government. While they are at it, the university should give David Duke an award for tolerance.

If we are talking about mendacity from a sitting president, Obama has no equal. During his tenure in the White House, he surpassed even inveterate liars like the Clintons. Thanks to Jonathan Gruber, one of the architects of Obamacare, we know that Obama deliberately covered up the truth about his signature health legislation. His most infamous lie was the oft-repeated promise that, "If you like your plan, you can keep your plan." An article in the *Chicago Tribune* summed it up: "Smug Obama Administration Duped the Public."

Obama also promised "no tax increases." The 2012 Supreme Court ruling that Obamacare's individual mandate is a tax means that the law violated the president's pledge not to raise taxes on middle class and poor Americans. According to the Senate Budget Committee, "President Obama has imposed one of the largest tax hikes in American history on the middle class."

His anti-war rhetoric that, "The global war on terror is over," was another attempt to mislead the American public with a carefully worded campaign of misinformation. Obama tried to take the focus off of his ineffectual response to terrorism by saying, "No challenge poses a greater risk ... than climate change." Jeb Bush responded by saying, "That is perhaps the most ludicrous comment I've ever heard, that climate change is a bigger threat to our country than Islamic terrorism." Political commentator Charles Krauthammer agreed, saying, "What planet is the president living on?"

And of course, we have this stalwart misrepresentation: "The economy is getting stronger ... confidence is growing." Obama's policies of higher taxes and over-regulation had a disastrous effect on the economy. All the leading economic indicators showed decline under Obama's anti-business onslaught. *The Federalist* concluded that Obama "has presided over the slowest, weakest economic recovery since the Great Depression."

In spite of his awful record, Obama thinks he should get all the credit for the economic resurgence that is happening during Trump's presidency. Obama predicted the economy would *never* grow above two percent. After Trump lowered taxes and began overturning Obama's regulations, the economy jumped to over four percent. Commenting on this aspect of Obama's speech, Sen. Lindsay Graham tweeted, "The more former President Obama speaks about the 'good ol years' of his presidency, the more likely President Trump is to get re-elected."

Clash Daily, September 13, 2018

Chapter 3: Hillary

Will Big Sister Be Watching You in 2017?

George Orwell's famous novel, *Nineteen Eighty-Four*, envisioned a totalitarian future where Big Brother will be watching everything you do. Well guess what? Orwell got it right...except for the gender. If HRC gets in on November 8, pack up the Constitution along with the Bill of Rights and make room for BIG SISTER!

During the past eight years, we have stood by as Obama thumbed his nose at Congress in order to expand the executive branch at the expense of individual rights, the private sector, and national security. The Obama/Clinton cabal has already compromised the Justice Department, the IRS, and the FBI. Big Sister, who has openly expressed disdain for the voting public, will push the envelope much further. She will appoint "progressive" Supreme Court justices who will condone her illegal efforts to sabotage the republic.

The worst part of it will be the suppression of the First Amendment. The Democrats have already begun to silence anyone who denies global warming, criticizes Islamic terrorism, or advocates a stronger military. Once Big Sister gets away with censoring what we can and can't say on these issues, she will have a clear path to outlawing ANY opinions that contradict those of her highness. Recent laws passed in Congress authorize the detention and torture of American citizens who are suspected of having ties to terrorist organizations. These laws could easily be expanded to include anyone who disagrees with Big Sister. And having lost free speech, we will have lost everything.

Big Sister's ideology is straight out of Lenin, Mao, and Alinsky. Take it away from those who have and give it to those who have not earned it. When Obama said he was for redistribution of income, we didn't believe he really meant it. HRC said she wants to raise taxes so she can satisfy the voracious appetite of the already obese federal government. Believe her. She means it.

We are at a crucial moment in our history in which the government is insinuating itself into every facet of our lives. Social mores are being torn apart. The press is no longer free to express contrary viewpoints. Universities are becoming "safe spaces" where only progressive liberal points of view are acceptable. Children are informing on their parents. The productive segment of the population is being demonized so "protected" classes can assert their entitlements.

On top of all that, Big Sister wants to open the borders to anyone who wants to come, including unvetted "refugees" from the Middle East. Big Sister will see to it that all immigrants receive generous financial entitlements so they will vote Democrat and erase forever the two-party system. After eliminating the two-term limit for president, Big Sister will be free to dictate over our lives for many years ahead.

Big Sister portends disaster. But of course none of that matters because Donald Trump is a "sexual predator." *Have we lost our minds?*

Daily Surge, October 16, 2016

Clinton's Strategy: Going for the Cheap Shot

When you have nothing positive going for you on the issues, distract the voting public by burying your opponent with personal attacks. Sound familiar? President Obama implied in his 2016 State of the Union address that Donald Trump is a racist. In keeping with her intention to become a third Obama term, Hillary Clinton adopted Obama's *ad hominem* attack as the leading edge of her presidential campaign.

Here is the *Wikipedia* definition of *ad hominem*: "A logical fallacy in which an argument is rebutted by attacking the character, motive, or other attribute of the person making the argument rather than attacking the substance of the argument itself." Bill O'Reilly explains it: "The only chance that the Democrats have to win the White House is to say to the American public, 'These Republicans are racists.' The Democrats can't run on national security, they can't run on the economy, so they have to run on emotion."

Hillary Clinton does not want to discuss her open borders policy, her intention to raise taxes, or the pay-for-play corruption centering around her foundation. Instead, she continues to allege that Trump is a "sexual predator" based on an 11-year-old video that has been taken out of context. Following Big Sister around is her neurotic alter ego, Elizabeth Warren, who screams at Trump, "We've had it with guys like you!" Demonizing Donald with a pejorative label such as *racist* or *fascist* or *sexist* avoids the responsibility of actually responding in a meaningful way to the substance of his positions. Ironically this is what fascists do and it lowers the election to a disturbing level of depravity.

Adding immeasurably to her offense is the hypocrisy of Big Sister's arguments. HRC is guilty of virtually every crime she tries to pin on Trump. Here are some examples:

• *Trump is racist* (because he wants to build the wall): While serving in the Senate, HRC voted to—guess what—*build a wall*. First Lady HRC called young black men "super-predators" implying that all young black males are violent criminals. She referred to a Jewish campaign operative as a "fucking Jew bastard."

• *Trump is sexist*: As reported in the *New York Post*, HRC is "waging the most sexist campaign in the history of presidential contests." Unashamedly playing the women's card, Big Sister has boasted that she has "a lot of experience dealing with men who sometimes get off the reservation." And let's not forget that she reputedly was the brains behind efforts to quell the "bimbo eruptions" that threatened to derail Bill's first presidential campaign.

• *Trump is bigoted*: *WikiLeaks* has revealed that Clinton does not think very highly of Southerners, Catholics, Evangelicals, and "needy" Hispanics.

• *Trump is in bed with Putin*: *WikiLeaks* has revealed that Big Sister's campaign manager, John Podesta, may have deep ties to Putin. And to top it off, there is the scandalous Clinton Foundation uranium deal that gives Russia control of 20 percent of America's uranium.

• *Trump won't release his taxes*: HRC won't release the content of her lucrative speeches to Wall Street.

• *Trump doesn't believe in equal pay*: According to the most recent figures, the Clinton Foundation leadership team has an $81,000 average gender pay gap.

And so it goes. Lie through the teeth. Big Sister will do anything in the pursuit of power. Unfortunately, the media is complicit in her ad hominem strategy. Newt Gingrich has observed that one night the networks spent 23 minutes on personal allegations against Trump versus a total of 56 seconds about HRC's dream of a borderless Western Hemisphere. I particularly enjoyed Gingrich's dressing down of Megan Kelly on Fox. "You are fascinated with sex and you don't care about public policy," Gingrich said. "I'm sick and tired of people like you using language that's inflammatory and not true. That's exactly the bias people are upset by." I'm glad somebody finally had the courage to say it.

Daily Surge, October 21, 2016

Hillary—The Sociopath Who Would Be President

It has been estimated that one in 25 Americans is a sociopath. As described by Dr. Martha Stout in *The Sociopath Next Door*, a sociopath is a person who lacks a conscience and whose behavior is marked by deceitfulness, irritability, and lack of remorse or responsibility when causing harm to others.

"Not everyone has a conscience," Dr. Stout explains. "Some people will never experience the exquisite angst that results from letting others down, or hurting them, or depriving them, or even killing them." Sociopaths are often charming and charismatic, but their main concern is for themselves and they often blame others for the things that they do. They have a complete disregard for rules and lie constantly. "It is not that this group fails to grasp the difference between good and bad," says Dr. Stout, "it is that the distinction fails to limit their behavior. Without the slightest blip of guilt or remorse, *one in 25 people can do anything at all.*" Hillary Rodham Clinton fits the profile perfectly, especially this trait: a grandiose sense of self-worth, as in, "Someday the world will realize how special I am." Sound familiar?

Clinton's persona is notable for the lack of a moral center, which is the defining characteristic of sociopaths. A penchant for not accepting responsibility has been observable throughout her public career. In her email server scandal, Clinton has acted as though she is above the law. When four Americans were murdered on her watch in the Benghazi disaster, Clinton defended herself by saying, "What difference does it make?" As secretary of state, she traded government favors for contributions to the Clinton Foundation and then lied about it. This week, Mrs. Clinton has done it again. Fox News reported that when questioned about the Harvey Weinstein scandal, she said, "This kind of behavior cannot be tolerated anywhere, whether it's in entertainment or politics." But when asked about the allegations of sexual predation made against Bill Clinton by numerous women—Juanita Broaddrick, Kathleen Willey, Paula Jones, and others—her evasive response was, "That has all been litigated. That was the subject of a huge investigation in the late 90s and there were conclusions drawn. That was clearly in the past."

The question I wanted the interviewer to put to Mrs. Clinton was this: "How do you distinguish between Harvey Weinstein using his power and influence to take advantage of a 23-year-old actress and Bill Clinton using his power and influence to take advantage of a 23-year-old intern?" Clearly, they are indistinguishable. If anything, Bill's behavior was worse because we have a right to expect more from the president than we do from a Hollywood producer. Not so for Mrs. Clinton. Weinstein's behavior is intolerable, she says, but the same behavior when applied to her husband apparently is not. Mrs. Clinton is a champion when it comes to reinterpreting the facts to suit her personal agenda.

Devious as this may be, something much more troubling can be found in Mrs. Clinton's interview. She managed to sneak in the accusation that, "After all, we have someone admitting to being a sexual assaulter in the Oval Office." My first reaction was, "Is she speaking about her husband? No. It can't be." Then I realized that she was referring to Donald Trump, flushing him down the same toilet as Harvey Weinstein while giving "Slick Willie" a complete pass. According to Mrs. Clinton—who came very close to becoming the sociopath in the White House—Trump is guilty of sexual assault. This is an out-and-out lie. The sole justification for Clinton's accusation was the *Access Hollywood* tape in which Trump's off-color remarks, for which he has apologized, did not include any admission of sexual assault. But Mrs. Clinton didn't allow the facts to interfere with her version of events any more than she did when she claimed that she came under sniper fire in Bosnia. It is significant to note that while Fox reported Mrs. Clinton's accusation against Trump, *a similar CNN story did not mention it at all.*

The hypocrisy of her self-anointed role as defender of women is exposed when she defends her husband's sex crimes. Covering up her husband's vile behavior and falsely accusing Donald Trump are manifestations of Mrs. Clinton's sociopathology, as is the attempt to blame her election loss on everyone else from Trump to the media to the Russians. By extension, the same can be said of the Democratic Party, a party that has consistently lied about its suppression of minorities and its contempt for the US Constitution. Democrats live by the Machiavellian adage of "the end justifies the means." The self-serving behavior of party apparatchiks like Chuck Schumer and Nancy Pelosi is devoid of a moral center.

"Sociopaths are almost invariably seen as bad or diabolical by mental health professionals," says Dr. Stout. "Not to care at all about the effects of our actions on friends, on family, on our children? What on earth would that be like?" The answer: It would be like Hillary Clinton. While it may be difficult to accept that sociopaths like Mrs. Clinton inhabit positions of power, it offers all the more reason why we need to identify them and seek protection from their amoral behavior.

Clash Daily, October 16, 2017

Part Two: Values

"If liberty means anything at all, it means the right to tell people what they do not want to hear."

George Orwell

Chapter 4: Free Speech v. Political Correctness

Free Speech is Dead in Europe—Are We Next?

All rights, including freedom of religion, stem from freedom of speech. Without free speech, we have nothing. Zero. The European Court of Human Rights has just dealt a death blow to freedom of speech in Europe. The ECHR decided that when an Austrian woman was convicted for criticizing the tenets of Islam, her right to free speech was not violated. The *Wall Street Journal* reported:

> *"Europe's highest human rights court ruled on Friday that disparagement of religious doctrines such as insulting the Prophet Muhammad isn't protected by freedom of expression and can be prosecuted."*

In 2009, an Austrian woman said that the Prophet Muhammed's marriage to a six-year-old girl was tantamount to pedophilia. Muhammad "liked to do it with children," she said, adding that, "A 56-year-old and a 6-year-old? What do we call it, if it is not pedophilia?" She claimed that her statement was protected by freedom of speech and that religious groups must tolerate criticism. The court in Vienna disagreed. She was convicted of disparaging religious doctrines and fined 480 Euros ($546).

In upholding the lower court's verdict, the European Court of Human Rights ruled that the right not to be offended is a more important right than freedom of expression. The Austrian court, said the ECHR, had "carefully balanced her right to freedom of expression with the right of others to have their religious feelings protected."

The ECHR has reinforced "hate speech" laws that prohibit criticism of religion in many European countries. Freedom of speech is restricted where religious feelings are involved, especially if the religion happens to be Islam. When other religions are criticized, the courts look the other way. Tucker Carlson on *Fox News* has correctly pointed out that the latest ECHR ruling effectively imposes Islamic blasphemy laws on the European continent. Such laws are inconsistent with the European tradition of free speech. Carlson also suggested that the ECHR has provided encouragement for Muslim terrorists such as the Charlie Hebdo shooters.

For several years, I have followed the career of Dutch politician Geert Wilders, a strong critic of Islamic immigration. After Wilders suggested last year that there are too many Moroccan immigrants in the Netherlands, he was convicted by a Dutch court of "insulting a group and inciting discrimination." Wilders reacted by saying that, "The Netherlands has become a sick country. You have restricted the freedom of speech for millions of Dutch."

What these restrictive court decisions are actually doing is masking a reluctance on the part of European countries to acknowledge the threat posed by Muslim immigration. The open border policy in the Netherlands, for example, has spawned dozens of crime-ridden "no-go" zones throughout Holland because so many of the Muslim immigrants refuse to assimilate. The same scenario is occurring in France, Belgium, the UK, Austria, Denmark, Sweden, Germany, Italy, and Spain.

The winner in this controversy is Islam. When freedom of speech is curtailed because Muslims complain they are being offended, it plays into what is known as "civilizational jihad"— the attempt to transform Western societies so they can be brought under the control of Islamic law, known as sharia. Sharia does not recognize freedom of speech, nor does it accept any concept of individual rights as embraced by the West. The self-destructive policies of European countries, led by Angela Merkel's open door policy in Germany, are collaborating with the Muslim hardliners who seek to destroy Western Civilization.

There is another dangerous implication in the European court's decision. If followed to its logical conclusion, anyone can claim that another person's speech is offensive and ought to be prohibited. Free speech is under attack because of two flawed ideas: political correctness and "emotional reasoning." The concept of political correctness, advocated by the Left, is a way of stifling free expression in favor of socially controlled thought. Emotional reasoning is where feelings determine the interpretation of reality. If someone is upset, that proves something is wrong. Under this doctrine, free speech does not apply if someone is offended.

Emotional reasoning has taken over American college campuses. "The belief that free speech rights don't include the right to speak offensively is now firmly entrenched on campuses and enforced by repressive speech or harassment codes," wrote attorney Wendy Kaminer in *The Atlantic*. Emotional reasoning has given birth to a slew of neurotic concepts, including microaggressions, free speech zones, safe spaces, trigger warnings, and hostile environments.

In a poll of 800 undergraduates conducted by McLaughlin & Associates, a majority of students favored codes limiting free speech. Campus authorities "are creating what tort law calls 'eggshell plaintiffs,'" wrote author Heather Mac Donald in *City Journal*. "Preternaturally fragile individuals injured by the slightest collisions with life. The consequences will affect us for years to come." These eggshell plaintiffs will be running the country in another generation.

Where will these trends lead? As the late author Christopher Hitchens said, "Freedom of speech must include the license to offend." I am offended, he said, "by those who claim the right not just to be offended but to seek violent reprisal as is so vividly being done by the votaries of the Prophet Muhammed." According to a poll by Wenzel Strategies, 58 percent of Muslim-Americans believe criticism of Islam is not protected free speech under the First Amendment. "To learn who rules over you," said Voltaire, "simply find out who you are not allowed to criticize."

Clash Daily, October 29, 2018

Too Bad If You're Offended—The Assault on Free Speech

Freedom of speech is coming under attack from all directions. The primary assault is based on the existence of a new "right": the right not to be offended. It is claimed by many that the right not to be offended is more important than the right to free expression.

Our colleges and universities have fallen victim to this new "right." The feelings of students often constitute sufficient justification for campus censorship. If a conservative speaker offends some of the students, that speaker can be denied a platform. "The belief that free speech rights don't include the right to speak offensively is now firmly entrenched on campuses and enforced by repressive speech or harassment codes," wrote attorney Wendy Kaminer in *The Atlantic*.

The problem is spreading to the mainstream. In the 2010 case of *Nurre v. Whitehead*, the U.S. Supreme Court upheld lower court rulings that school authorities can deny students' rights to free speech just to keep other students from being offended. The courts are "allowing schools the discretion to let an offended minority control a cowed majority," constitutional attorney John W. Whitehead wrote in *Huffington Post*. "There is no way to completely avoid giving offense," he said. "At some time or other, someone is going to take offense at something someone else says or does. It's inevitable. Such politically correct thinking has resulted in a host of inane actions, from the Easter Bunny being renamed 'Peter Rabbit' to Christmas Concerts being dubbed 'Winter' Concerts."

In a democracy, there can be no right not to be offended. If anyone can claim that another person's speech is offensive and ought to be prohibited, there is no limit to the restrictions that can be placed on free expression. As the late author Christopher Hitchens said, "Freedom of speech must include the license to offend." Wherever it is sanctioned, the "right" not to be offended invalidates the Bill of Rights and the Constitution. The difference between the U.S. and Cuba has to do with the right to say and think whatever you like even if someone is offended by it. "What protects people's rights to say things I find objectionable," Jodie Ginsburg wrote in *The Guardian*, "is precisely what protects my right to object."

"Nobody has the right to not be offended," said Salman Rushdie, the author targeted for murder by Islamic authorities that were offended by his novels. "That right doesn't exist in any declaration I have ever read. If you are offended it is your problem, and frankly lots of things offend lots of people."

In a well-publicized media interview, Canadian psychology professor Jordan B. Peterson was asked why his right to freedom of speech should take priority over a person's right not to be offended. "Because," he answered, "in order to be able to think, you have to risk being offensive." Then he added, "You're certainly willing to risk offending me in the pursuit of truth." The interviewer was stopped dead in her tracks by Peterson's astute reply.

The basis for the "I'm offended" movement lies in two flawed concepts: political correctness and "emotional reasoning." Political correctness is a way of stifling free expression in favor of socially controlled thought. Emotional reasoning is where feelings determine the interpretation of reality. If someone is upset, that proves something is wrong. It doesn't matter that you intended no disrespect. The subjective reaction of the other person determines the outcome. Under this doctrine, supported by the Left, free speech is an outdated concept.

The European Court of Human Rights just ruled that criticism of religion is not protected by freedom of speech and can be prosecuted if someone is offended. The ECHR has reinforced "hate speech" laws that prohibit criticism of religion in many European countries. Freedom of speech is restricted where religious feelings are wounded, especially if the religion happens to be Islam. It would appear that Islamic blasphemy laws have found a home in Europe.

When freedom of speech is curtailed because Muslims complain they are being offended, it plays into what is known as "civilizational jihad"—the attempt to transform Western societies so they can be brought under the control of Islamic law, known as sharia. Sharia does not recognize freedom of speech, nor does it accept any concept of individual rights as embraced by the West.

In Canada, the Human Rights Commission has defined harassment as "any unwanted physical or verbal behaviour that offends or humiliates you." For example, it is now a violation of Canada's Human Rights and Criminal codes to use incorrect gender pronouns if it offends somebody who wants to be called Googoo instead of he or she.

The good news is that in the 2017 case of Matal v. Tam, the Supreme Court defended free speech. The unanimous decision was written by Justice Samuel Alito, who wrote the dissent in the Nurre case. "Speech may not be banned on the ground that it expresses ideas that offend," Alito wrote. "Speech that demeans on the basis of race, ethnicity, gender, religion, age, disability, or any other similar ground is hateful; but the proudest boast of our free speech jurisprudence is that we protect the freedom to express 'the thought that we hate.'" There may be hope for the First Amendment after all.

Eagle Rising, October 30, 2018

Return of the Blacklist: The Left Shuts Down Free Speech

It was only a matter of time. Mimicking McCarthyism's call to hate, the Left is demanding a blacklist of those who oppose its political ideology. Dani Rodrik, Professor of International Political Economy at the bastion of leftism, Harvard University, has urged the academic world to stop offering jobs or honors to anyone who has served in the Trump administration. This ought not to come as a surprise. It reflects what author Mark Levin calls "the fascist, totalitarian mindset that is modern academia."

Professor Rodrik insists that universities "should uphold both free inquiry and the values of liberal democracy." Then, in a clear demonstration of leftist hypocrisy, he insults those values by demanding that Trump's supporters be placed on a blacklist. They should be prohibited, he says, from receiving "even a semblance of honor or recognition" from "the gatekeepers of higher learning."

Rodrik, who advocates income redistribution and opposes the free market system, accuses Trump of running an "odious presidency … We do not, after all, have a normal administration that can be served honorably … Those who serve with him are necessarily tainted by the experience." No exceptions. "Having served in this 'odious' administration," as observed by *hotair.com*, "you should now be barred for life from any form of service in academia."

Like its fellow travelers, the *New York Times* and the Democratic Party, Harvard has lost its credibility. These organs of the Left have one thing in common—they are against free speech. In spite of Professor Rodrik's phony defense of "free inquiry," try to get hired at Harvard if you espouse conservative ideas. A respected poll has pegged liberal faculty at four-year colleges and universities at 87 percent. Another study identified Democrats to Republicans in journalism departments of 1,500 universities at 20-1, and a whopping 33.5-1 in history departments. Today's college campuses have become fueling stations for the Left.

How did this happen? According to Ben Shapiro, author of *Bullies: How the Left's Culture of Fear and Intimidation Silences Americans*, college administrators decided in the 1960s that it was "easier to appease rampaging leftist students than to deal with them. They came to an agreement with the wildebeests: stop taking over the buildings and locking the doors, and we'll start teaching you about how America sucks." Gradually that translated into liberalism becoming a prerequisite for getting hired. Many campuses require new faculty members to sign a diversity statement. "What diversity oaths seek," says Walter E. Williams, professor of economics at George Mason University, "is to maintain political conformity among the faculty indoctrinating our impressionable, intellectually immature young people. The last thing that diversity hustlers want," Williams concludes, "is diversity in ideas."

Intellectual freedom on campus is flirting with extinction. When I attended college, students demanded more freedom of expression. Today's students, says Scott Greer in *No Campus for White Men*, demand less freedom and actually want to limit free expression. Political correctness on campus is giving rise to a new generation that is poised to throw free speech out the window. Activists believe that free speech is their exclusive province. Contrary opinions are oppressive and labeled as hate speech. "Campus leftists," says Greer, "are able to suppress all dissenting speech for the supposed good of mankind."

Academia has "invented a labyrinth of anti-free speech tools," says political commentator Kirsten Powers, that are "weapons to silence anyone who expresses a view that deviates from the left's worldview or ideology." George Orwell warned about this problem in *Nineteen Eighty-Four*. The U.S. experienced a taste of it in the 1950s as McCarthyism tried to shut down the Left. Now the Left is getting revenge by attempting to silence the Right.

Because Harvard wields a great deal of influence, Rodrik's proposal will be taken seriously by other campuses around the country—most of which are controlled by the Left. What can be done to prevent an intercollegiate blacklist? David Horowitz, author of *Big Agenda: President Trump's Plan to Save America*, urges a campaign that will force universities to add "intellectual and political diversity" into their mission statements. This might compel them to hire conservative professors for a long overdue change.

The alternative is a disturbing view of the possible social and political discourse in America's future. If academia imposes a blacklist on conservatives, will the corporate world and government agencies be next? The kids marching today to shut down Trump supporters or anyone else they don't like, says Scott Greer, could very well be the senators, judges, and newspaper editors of tomorrow. "Give me four years to teach the children," said Lenin, "and the seed I have sown will never be uprooted."

American Thinker, August 18, 2018

The Strange Death of Individual Liberties

All individual rights, including freedom of religion, stem from freedom of speech and freedom of the press. Without the two of them, we have nothing. Both of these concepts have been bequeathed to the United States by the tradition of common law that evolved in England over a thousand-year period. We owe a tremendous debt to the Anglo-Saxon/Norman legal tradition. In a strange and perverse development, a concerted attack on individual liberties is being waged by politicians in the UK. The birthplace of our legal traditions is turning into a police state.

Let me put the situation in perspective. For more than ten years, gangs of Muslim men have raped thousands—that's right, THOUSANDS—of young, often underage, white girls in towns in the north of England. The government in the UK has been reluctant to acknowledge the existence of these gangs, known euphemistically as "Asian grooming gangs." They are in reality Muslim rape gangs. The police do not arrest them and the courts do not prosecute them. The government discourages criticism of its immigration policies and labels dissenters as racists. Many cases remain unreported because victims are often ostracized by their communities if they go public with allegations of abuse. Douglas Murray, British author of *The Strange Death of Europe*, commented on the disgraceful crisis in *National Review*:

> *"For years the British state allowed gangs of men to rape thousands of young girls across Britain. For years the police, politicians, Crown Prosecution Service, and every other arm of the state ostensibly dedicated to protecting these girls failed them. As a number of government inquires have concluded, they turned their face away from these girls because they were terrified*

*of the accusations of racism that would come their way
if they did address them. They decided it wasn't worth
the aggravation."*

Tommy Robinson, a controversial conservative activist, did not turn away. He attempted to expose the failure of British justice and was punished for it. Robinson was arrested a week ago for snapping photos of defendants in a rape trial as they entered a courthouse in Leeds, England. In the tiny space of five hours, Robinson was surrounded by police, arrested, tried, convicted, and sentenced to 13 months in jail. It has taken years for the British legal system to bring the Muslim rape gangs to justice but Robinson was given his justice in a few hours. "Where was the swift justice for the victims of the grooming gangs?" asks irate British journalist Katie Hopkins. Robinson "has been treated with greater suspicion and a greater presumption of guilt by the United Kingdom," says Douglas Murray, "than any Islamic extremist or mass rapist ever has been."

Robinson was thrown in prison because the British justice system has ruled that reporting on the rape trials is illegal. It also ruled that reporting on Robinson's arrest is illegal. Douglas Murray expresses his fear of being prosecuted for writing about Robinson in *National Review*, even though it is not a British publication. This contempt for freedom of speech and the press is a warning to America. "Britain used to be a bastion of free speech," lamented Dutch conservative politician Geert Wilders. "Today its leaders are behaving like North Korea and Saudi Arabia."

Instead of defending freedom of the press, the mainstream UK media are celebrating Tommy Robinson's conviction. "It is more important for them to be seen as multicultural and accepting and welcoming to our Muslim colleagues and friends," says Katie Hopkins, "than to stand up for what is right." What does this amount to? "We no longer have freedom of speech," says Hopkins. "These are very dark times for the UK. The country is on a knife edge. There is a real sense now that we are against our own government, that the establishment is working against us and in order to cleanse voices it doesn't like, it will put them inside for as long as it takes to shut them up."

As in other parts of Europe, the UK has strong "hate speech" laws. The penalties for hate speech include fines, imprisonment, or both. For practical purposes, "hate speech" includes anything critical of the Islamic religion, Muslim immigration, or Muslims. Criticize Muslim "grooming gangs" and you will be put behind bars. In effect, Islamic blasphemy laws are now the law of the land in the UK. And so you have the cruel fate of Tommy Robinson, who faces assault by Muslim gangs inside the prison where he will spend the next year of his life while Muslim rape gangs are free to poison the towns and villages of England with their heinous crimes.

Thousands of angry Brits marched last week in support of Robinson. Not only are individual freedoms being trampled upon, elected politicians are ignoring the voices of their constituents. Unfortunately, the same impetus that drives the UK to trash its most treasured liberties is alive and well in the US. For some time, the Democratic Party has engaged in a campaign to destroy the First Amendment. Free speech is regarded by the American Left as an outdated concept. "People who defend and extol free speech," says author and psychologist Jordan Peterson, "tend to be branded as right-wingers." Mark Steyn, author of *America Alone*, observed that we are turning into "one vast college campus" where there is one politically correct view and all others are prohibited.

How long will it be before Democratic politicians introduce bills designed to eviscerate the First Amendment? How long before we are prohibited from criticizing illegal immigration or Islamic terrorism or climate change? It has already begun in left-leaning states like California. If it can happen in the UK, it can happen here. We must defend our constitutional rights and privileges before we too become a police state. Our voices must be heard.

Lantern of Liberty, June 3, 2018

Chapter 5: Due Process and the Rule of Law

Impeachment Show Trial—Shades of Stalin

In the 1930s Soviet Union, Joseph Stalin conducted a series of trials designed to eliminate his political opponents. All charges were fabricated. The guilt of the defendants was established before the trial. Confessions were extracted using torture and threats. They were called "show trials" because Stalin wanted to create the impression that the defendants were being tried fairly. No one was naïve enough to believe that these were fair trials. No one could have predicted that the same thing would occur in the US, yet we are now witnessing what amounts to a show trial of the president.

From the first day of Trump's landing in the Oval Office, the Democrats—with the complicity of the Deep State and the media—have attempted to sabotage his presidency. It began with the Mueller investigation, which was what I called at the time the "Mt. Everest of political diversions." The Mueller probe was an effort to divert attention from the worst political scandal in American history—a multitude of criminal activities by the DNC, the Hillary Clinton campaign, and members of the Obama administration including but not limited to Hillary Clinton, James Comey, Loretta Lynch, Susan Rice, and Obama himself. Mueller's efforts met the same fate as Hillary's presidential hopes, i.e., they failed miserably, much to the chagrin of Nancy Pelosi, Chuck Schumer, and company.

The Democrats were not discouraged by the failure of the special counsel. Pelosi threatened to up the pressure on Trump if the Democrats won back the House, which they did. Their next big gambit was to stage an impeachment, which also was a diversion—in this case an attempt to divert attention from the crimes committed by the leading Democratic candidate for the 2020 presidential race, Uncle Joe Biden. By his own admission—on video, no less—Biden committed extortion against the Ukrainian government. Biden threatened to withhold a billion dollars of US aid if Ukraine's president didn't fire a prosecutor who was investigating the lucrative sweetheart deal given to Biden's son, Hunter.

Thanks in large part to Peter Schweizer's eye-opening book, "Secret Empires: How the American Political Class Hides Corruption and Enriches Family and Friends," we know that Biden used his position as vice president to enrich his son. That is called corruption. The Democrats want to impeach Trump because he wants to investigate that corruption. You can't make this up.

Enter Adam Schiff and his show trial. No one is quite sure what "high crimes and misdemeanors" have been committed by the president that would justify impeachment. As in Stalin's trials, the emperor has no clothes. "Nothing we have heard establishes a claim that the president acted improperly," says Rep. Devin Nunes, "and nothing has been presented to support anything near impeachment."

The original hearings were conducted in secret, hidden away in a basement. Republicans were not allowed. Now that Schiff has admitted Devin Nunes and Jim Jordan to the proceedings, Schiff is showing contempt for due process by arbitrarily placing limits on what the Republicans can say and do. "He doesn't want his narrative to be challenged," says Mark Levin. He only allows information that benefits the Democratic position. The Republicans are not allowed to present witnesses. Schiff's feeble witnesses claim to have direct knowledge of presidential misconduct when in fact they are only capable of promoting second, third, and fourth-hand hearsay. It doesn't matter. A five-year-old child can tell that the entire thing is a farce.

From the inception, Schiff has made up his own facts—including his own counterfeit version of Trump's phone call with Ukrainian President Zelensky. Schiff's arrogance is all the more outrageous when you consider that Trump had already released the actual transcript. What I don't understand, however, is how the Democrats can be stupid enough not to realize that (a) the American public can see through the farcical nature of the entire proceeding, and (b) their impeachment argument will be destroyed if it ever goes to the Senate.

More than that, Schiff's circus is an assumption of tyrannical powers in order to invalidate a bona fide presidential election. "What you are witnessing is tyranny," says Mark Levin. "This is an outrageous violation of the Constitution." Why are the Democrats doing this? Levin believes that their real aim is to influence the 2020 election. He also underscores the role of the media: "They sound like the Russian media! None of the newsrooms is calling it straight."

"There is only one way to fix this," says Levin. "On election day." A satisfying consolation is that the Democrats will get their just deserts at the ballot box.

Clash Daily, November 22, 2019

The 28th Amendment

We are witnessing the rise of a new "right" which, if liberals had prevailed in the recent election, might have been glorified in the form of a constitutional amendment. It would read something like this:

> *"The 28th Amendment: A state, city, or individual may choose which laws they wish to obey and which laws they wish to disregard without risk of legal consequences."*

For example, let's say that the mayor of New York City decides that murder is no longer a crime. "If you commit murder in Chicago," the mayor might declare, "come to New York and you will not be prosecuted." Or let's consider the possibility, as hypothesized by Mark Levin, that anyone who commits murder will be exonerated if they are raising a family. "New Yorkers value the importance of family over all other considerations. When you commit murder in New York, you will not be prosecuted if you can demonstrate that you are raising a family."

Sounds completely insane, don't you agree? But this is exactly what is happening with "sanctuary cities." The mayors of New York, Chicago, San Francisco, and many other cities have decided that they are not obliged to enforce federal immigration laws. Undocumented aliens will not be challenged by local law enforcement nor will such persons be turned over to federal authorities as required by law, even if that person is a felon. Sanctuary cities oppose Kate's Law, which would impose mandatory harsh sentences against undocumented immigrants who commit felonies. And why do they support the defiance of federal immigration laws? On the grounds that people who break these laws are trying to raise their families and we just can't destroy the sanctity of the family. *Hallelujah!*

On today's *O'Reilly Factor*, a guest argued that sanctuary cities are justified because immigrants contribute to our society. When it was pointed out that many immigrants are here illegally, the response was the usual doubletalk that attempts to sidestep the legal issue altogether. The problem we face, like it or not, is that when it becomes acceptable to disobey one law, the door is opened for disobeying all laws. If you can enter the country illegally without consequences, then why can't you commit murder or any other crime without consequences?

Our elected public officials take an oath to defend our system of laws. It is irresponsible and criminal when they encourage disrespect for the laws they are sworn to defend. It all starts at the top. President Obama, reacting to the violent protests after the recent election, refused to speak out against the violence. Instead, he actually encouraged people to continue to break the law. If the president can do this, why can't a mayor or a governor? What kind of precedent is being set?

The solution for progressives is the 28th Amendment. Let's institutionalize anarchy. That may sound like a contradiction in terms, but anarchy is what we are going to have if the rule of law is ignored. We can't have it both ways. Either we are a country of laws or we are nothing.

Daily Surge, November 22, 2016

Mueller Investigation: The Mt. Everest of Political Diversions

When Donald Trump announced that he wanted to drain the swamp, he triggered the most intensive backlash since Moses parted the Red Sea. Everyone with a hand in the till rose up to destroy the new president in order to protect vested interests. The Democratic Party. Obama appointees aka the "Deep State." Washington lobbyists. Republicans with their own little fiefdoms. A staggering array of antagonists who would stop at nothing to delegitimize the Trump presidency. Their collective scheming came up with a diabolical strategy: the special counsel.

The narrative began with an unsubstantiated allegation that the Trump campaign had colluded with "the Russians." What would we do without the Russians? It is always convenient to have a rotten villain upon whom you can blame everything. This is nothing new to Washington. The Russians were used for a similar purpose 60 years ago by Sen. Joe McCarthy. In 2017 it probably would have stopped at the insinuation stage except for one little wrinkle. The newly appointed attorney general, Jeff Sessions, decided to recuse himself from the Russian issue. He probably didn't have to since the allegation was bogus, but he did.

"Since I had involvement with the campaign," Sessions said, "I should not be involved in any campaign investigation." Trump knew this spelled trouble. "Sessions should have never recused himself," said the president, "and if he was going to recuse himself, he should have told me before he took the job and I would have picked somebody else." Point well taken, Mr. President, but it's too late now.

The man who took the ball from Sessions, Deputy Attorney General Rod Rosenstein, appointed Robert Mueller as special counsel to investigate the allegations of collusion. The selection of Mueller at that particular time was significant because the president had just fired James Comey from his post as FBI director, and it seems that Mueller and Comey were buddies from way back. Mueller hired a huge staff of mainly Trump-haters. The farcical investigation has continued for a year despite the lack of evidence of Trump-Russia collusion. How can that be justified? It seems that Mueller is not going to be thwarted by the absence of evidence. He is going to find Trump guilty of something if it kills him. The plot of a bad novel, perhaps?

In the meantime, Rep. Devin Nunes of the House Intelligence Committee has introduced evidence that the Justice Department and the FBI colluded with the Clinton campaign, the DNC, and *the Russians* to interfere with the 2016 presidential election. The truth is finally coming out. The Mueller investigation appears to have been nothing more than an effort to divert attention from the worst political scandal in American history—a multitude of criminal activities by members of the Obama administration including but not limited to Hillary Clinton, Loretta Lynch, Susan Rice, and Obama himself. It looks like there was collusion with the Russians, only it was the Democrats who did it. We desperately need a special counsel—to investigate the illegal activities of the Democrats, not the Republicans.

Those wily Democrats succeeded in diverting attention from themselves by stoking the fire under the Mueller investigation. Clever? Without question. Diabolical? In light of the emerging facts, without a doubt. And yet no one talks about it, least of all the mainstream media that used to be the guardian of the truth. That function has devolved upon Fox News and conservative talk radio. People like Mark Levin and Sean Hannity talk about it every day, but no one seems to be listening.

We have cooked up a witch hunt against the wrong people. It is a complete miscarriage of justice, a national disgrace. Trump may have a lot of faults, but he did not collude with the Russians and he did not try to use the intelligence apparatus of the United States to subvert a legitimate presidential election. It's time we faced the music and went after the real traitors and felons. If we don't, say goodbye to the American justice system. In addition to all the other statues that are up for grabs, we better tear down the statue of justice. Remember that one? A blindfolded woman holding a set of scales? She will be sorely missed.

Clash Daily, February 19, 2018

The Deep State Cabal Against Trump

"When those who are entrusted to enforce the law," says author and Fox News host Gregg Jarrett, "instead, abuse their power to pursue innocent people in the name of justice it is the worst kind of oppression." The special counsel investigation—into alleged collusion between the Trump campaign and the Russians to influence the 2016 election—is the quintessence of such oppression. "There was never any real evidence of wrongdoing," Jarrett writes in his excellent new book, *The Russia Hoax: The Illicit Scheme to Clear Hillary Clinton and Frame Donald Trump.* "In the absence of credible allegations or information that a specific law was broken," he argues, "the probe was unlawful."

Author Mark Levin reminds us of the irony in the current situation. "Hillary Clinton, Bill Clinton, and Christopher Steele all have a clear connection to the Russians," says Levin. "The only person who does not have any connection to the Russians is Trump and he's the one they are trying to take down." The Trump-Russia collusion story was manufactured by bureaucrats whose "motives were impure," says Jarrett, "animated by antipathy for Trump." As part of the swamp, they need to protect themselves from the man who has sworn to drain it.

The initial goal of this scheme by top officials of the FBI and Obama's Justice Department was the protection and then election of Hillary Clinton. We know from reading the emails of Peter Strzok and Lisa Page that high-ranking members of the FBI were working behind the scenes to ensure the defeat of Donald Trump. When that failed, they launched their "Plan B"—the special counsel investigation. Former FBI Director James Comey, with the collaboration of Deputy Attorneys General Sally Yates and Rod Rosenstein, used an unverified dossier as the basis for the phony investigation and for spying on Trump and his campaign. Comey's worst offense was obtaining the special counsel appointment for his friend, Robert Mueller. Jarrett refers to this as "a devious maneuver by an unscrupulous man."

Call it a cabal, call it collusion, call it obstruction of justice, call it whatever you want. It all comes down to the same thing—criminal conspiracy by unelected members of the federal bureaucracy, the Deep State, to destroy Donald Trump's presidency. All of these people should be indicted for a long list of federal crimes. Mueller and Rosenstein should have recused themselves because of conflicts of interest. Instead, they used the investigation into alleged Trump-Russia collusion to prosecute Trump allies General Michael Flynn, Paul Manafort, and Robert Cohen. Although these prosecutions have nothing to do with the probe's original mandate, the motivation seems clear—squeezing them for information that will take down the president.

While this travesty makes a noisy splash in the partisan mainstream media, a guilty cast of characters from the Obama administration—Hillary Clinton, Susan Rice, John Brennan, Samantha Power, Loretta Lynch, Eric Holder, and Barack Obama himself—is going free. Jarrett spells out their crimes in agonizing detail. Why haven't they been investigated? The answer: the guilty parties are the same corrupt people who run the justice system. For justice to prevail, they would be required to investigate themselves. Attorney General Jeff Sessions could do it, but he is missing in action.

The cabal will continue as the Democrats, urged on by Nancy Pelosi, are planning a full-frontal assault to obstruct Trump's administration. According to *National Review*, if Democrats gain a congressional majority in the November elections we can expect them to block Trump's legislative agenda and his Supreme

Court nominees. Congressional committees led by Democrats will be "militantly focused on investigations" of the president, his staff, and agency appointees. "This will result in near-paralysis for the administration."

Collateral damage from this anti-Trump cabal includes the loss of confidence by the American public in our system of justice. If the powers of the federal government can be weaponized to sabotage a duly-elected president, what perversion of justice will be directed at you and me? What hope is there for the future of our individual rights? It is hard to believe, but America may have just moved one step closer to totalitarianism.

Media Equalizer, September 5, 2018

Nadler Launches Round Three of the Anti-Trump Cabal

In the wake of a fruitless two-year investigation of Donald Trump by the special counsel, House Judiciary Committee Chairman Jerry Nadler is launching the third round of the illegal cabal against the president. "For two years," Nadler said, "the Trump administration has been attacking the core functions of our democracy and the Congress has refused to do any oversight. We are going to find out, we are going to lay out the facts for the American people."

Nadler said he plans to request documents from more than 60 people linked to the president because, "It's our job to protect the rule of law. That's our core function," Nadler said. "And to do that we are going to initiate investigations into abuses of power, into corruption and into obstruction of justice."

Instead of laying out the facts, Nadler outed himself as a liar. First he alleged, "It's *very clear* that the president obstructed justice." Not conceivable, not possible, but "very clear." When asked how Trump has obstructed justice, Nadler gave this feeble reply: "It's very clear – 1,100 times he referred to the Mueller investigation as a witch hunt, he tried to protect Flynn from being investigated by the FBI. He fired Comey in order to stop the Russian thing. He's threatened – he's intimidated witnesses. In public."

Then Nadler contradicted his allegation with an outright admission that the evidence is not there. "We don't have the facts yet," he said, "but we're going to initiate proper investigations." We don't have the facts "yet"—implying that the facts surely must exist if only Nadler can discover them.

When asked if he would accept a finding by the Mueller team that there was no evidence of collusion, Nadler replied: "This investigation goes far beyond collusion. We've seen all the Democratic norms that we depend on for Democratic government attacked by the administration." Where is the proof, Jerry? Trump is the target of a politically motivated craving to bring down his administration. Nadler claims that his campaign against Trump is simply a search for the truth. Actually, it is a Stalinist effort to find wrongdoing even if none exists. The Democratic Party has levied an assault upon the Constitution by attempting to invalidate a bona fide presidential election.

Exposing the deception of Nadler's position, House Minority Leader Kevin McCarthy said on ABC's *This Week* that, "Congressman Nadler decided to impeach the president the day the president won the election." Actually, the cabal began prior to the 2016 election. As Fox News host Gregg Jarrett explains in *The Russia Hoax: The Illicit Scheme to Clear Hillary Clinton and Frame Donald Trump*, a criminal conspiracy was perpetrated by unelected members of the federal bureaucracy, the Deep State, in order to destroy Donald Trump's presidency. The first round of the cabal consisted of the scheme by top officials of the FBI and Obama's Justice Department for the protection and then election of Hillary Clinton. We know from reading the emails of Peter Strzok and Lisa Page that high-ranking members of the FBI were working behind the scenes to ensure the defeat of Donald Trump. When that failed, they launched round two of the cabal— the special counsel investigation, which has not lived up to their expectations.

The cabal continued last Fall as the Democrats, urged on by Nancy Pelosi, threatened a full-frontal assault to obstruct Trump's administration if they won control of the House in the midterm elections. The Dems are making good on their threat.

"This will result in near-paralysis for the administration," predicted the *National Review*.

Never a shrinking violet, the president lashed out against his detractors. "I am an innocent man," Trump tweeted, "being persecuted by some very bad, conflicted & corrupt people in a Witch Hunt that is illegal & should never have been allowed to start - And only because I won the Election!" He is absolutely correct. The Democrats have not recovered from Trump's election. As a political outsider sworn to "drain the swamp," the president scares the pants off the Washington elite. They will do anything to protect their lucrative rackets, whether their tactics are legal or not. "When those who are entrusted to enforce the law, instead, abuse their power to pursue innocent people in the name of justice it is the worst kind of oppression," Gregg Jarrett writes in *The Russia Hoax*.

The Democrats have no right to sabotage the Constitution just because they lost an election. The irony is that Nadler justifies his role in the anti-Trump cabal with the dubious argument that he is upholding the rule of law. Where were Nadler and his colleagues during eight years of abuses against the rule of law by the Obama administration? Hiding under a rock on Pennsylvania Avenue? It is proof that the Democratic Party worships a double standard.

While there is pressure from leftist groups for immediate impeachment of the president, the Democrats are "torn over what to do with it," suggests *Politico*, "fearful that their efforts will backfire and end up helping Trump." Public opinion may be on Trump's side. Nadler himself warned that Democrats should not risk being accused of subverting the will of the people. If you impeach Trump, he said, "you don't [want to] have half the country saying for the next 30 years: We won the election, you stole it."

Collateral damage from the anti-Trump cabal includes the loss of confidence by the American public in our system of justice. If the powers of the federal government can be weaponized to sabotage a duly-elected president, where will it lead? When a government doesn't have a crime but starts an investigation to find one, that's called a police state. It is hard to believe, but Nadler and his party may be moving America one step closer to the totalitarian world of George Orwell's *Nineteen Eighty-Four*. Beware—Big Brother Nadler is watching you.

Clash Daily, March 12, 2019

Liberty and Justice for All—All Democrats, That Is!

One of the underlying values of our country has always been the belief in justice and fair play. Wait a minute. Not true, say many African-Americans who have argued that justice has been denied them. America wears two faces, they insist. A double standard. Fortunately, that period of time has been relegated to history. The notion that blacks are victims of a racist society may have been true prior to the 1960s, but this is a half-century after the Civil Rights Movement. "White institutional racism has disappeared from our society," explains author Scott Greer in *No Campus for White Men*. "The oppression of black Americans is over with," African-American author Shelby Steele agreed during last week's *Life, Liberty and Levin* on Fox TV. That means America finally has justice and fairness, isn't that right? Unfortunately, no.

In the Age of Obama, the Democratic Party decided to substitute conservatives for blacks. Now it is conservatives who are being denied justice and fairness. If you agree with the liberal playbook, you get all the justice and fairness that money can buy. But if you are a conservative and a Trump supporter, you are subjected to a double standard. Sorry. Justice and fair play do not apply to you. Nothing proves this double standard more than the existence of the "cover-Hillary's-butt" team and the "kick-Trump-in-the-pants" campaign.

Hillary Clinton has been protected consistently by the justice system, from the Benghazi scandal to the uranium deal to the Clinton Foundation's money laundering scheme. The Justice Department and the FBI sunk to a new low by absolving Mrs. Clinton of guilt for violating the Espionage Act when she used a private server to transmit classified information and then destroyed the evidence. After spelling out her transgressions in excruciating detail, FBI Director Comey told us—with a straight face—that no charges would be filed against Mrs. Clinton because "no reasonable prosecutor would bring such a case."

But Paul Manafort, who may have done something questionable a dozen years ago, is placed in solitary confinement for months—without being convicted of a crime—because he is deemed guilty of being a Trump supporter. Fox News host Tucker Carlson announced that two sources confirmed to him that Tony Podesta, brother of Hillary's campaign manager, John Podesta, has been given immunity for the same alleged crimes that Manafort has been charged with. Manafort is being crucified while Clinton and her cronies walk away untouched.

Dinesh D'Souza, an outspoken conservative and critic of Obama, was locked up with violent criminals for eight months because he violated a minor campaign finance law for which previous offenders received a slap on the wrist. General Michael Flynn, Trump's first national security adviser, was coerced into pleading guilty of lying to the FBI, even though FBI Director Comey eventually testified that he did not believe that Flynn had lied. Once again, our respected FBI is complicit in the double standard.

And what about the campaign against Donald Trump? No president in my lifetime has faced such a vicious barrage of attacks from Democrats, Rinos, and the media. Barack Obama, a socialist who hates America, never faced anything like this. On the contrary, anyone who had the temerity to criticize Obama was automatically called out as a racist. Is this not a double standard?

"Russia collusion investigation"—are you kidding me? There is still no evidence for this, yet the nation has been torn apart by the unaccountable, partisan "special" prosecutor appointed by the Deep State to sabotage the Trump presidency. Democratic lawmakers feel free to recommend that you should go out of your way to assault Trump supporters wherever and whenever possible. A disturbed Bernie Sanders supporter attempted to massacre a baseball field full of Republican congressmen. When you put it all together, the case for a double standard is unavoidable.

Talk show host Glenn Beck and others, including the president, have accused the media of reinforcing the double standard. Can they possibly be correct? Of course they are. The media has abdicated its role as defender of the truth. They spend 90 percent of their time attacking Trump and his supporters in a contemporary version of McCarthyism. Every day, I have the misfortune of watching CNN when I work out at the gym. All I see is speculation and unsubstantiated conspiracy theories on why Trump is a racist, misogynist, and tyrant. Anything he is for they are against. It is impossible to believe anything that is broadcast on that channel. Jim Acosta of CNN harangued White House Press Secretary Sarah Sanders because he is upset that the president referred to the media as an enemy of the people. If the shoe fits, Mr. Acosta, wear it!

It would be nice to believe that we have finally grown into our own set of values. That justice and fair play are indeed American virtues. In view of the double standard practiced by the Democrats, the Deep State, and their media enablers, that is out of the question.

LifeZette, August 6, 2018

Should Professor Ford Be Applauded or Prosecuted?

Feminists have jumped on the Kavanaugh confirmation bandwagon in order to advocate the conviction of all men for the sexual assaults committed by a few men. Senators Feinstein, Harris, and Hirono "are saying because women have been assaulted, you can't vote for any man who has been accused," explains author and TV commentator Bill O'Reilly. "So therefore anybody can raise an accusation to disqualify anyone from an appointed position or even running for office." That is the very definition of witch hunt.

Is it important whether accusations of men by women are truthful? It doesn't matter, says Sen. Mazie Hirono of Hawaii. "Not only do women like Dr. Ford, who bravely comes forward, need to be heard," says Hirono, *"but they need to be believed."* Hirono expects all of the "enlightened men in our country" to rise up and say, "We cannot continue the victimization and the smearing of someone like Dr. Ford." Poor, poor Dr. Ford.

Poor, poor United States of America when due process and respect for the truth go flying out the window. We have always believed that a person is innocent until proven guilty. We have always believed that the burden of proof is on the accuser, not the accused. The Left wants to change all that when it is not convenient, as in the case of Judge Kavanaugh's confirmation to the Supreme Court. We can thank the Democrats for perverting our judicial system in support of their political objectives. The politically correct thing to do is (a) believe Ford by virtue of her sex and (b) place the burden on Kavanaugh to prove he didn't do it. Otherwise, say the Democrats, we could have a justice who might rule against progressive ideas like curtailing freedom of speech or replacing free markets with socialism.

Ford testified that her life has been ruined by the impact of a sexual assault. It took real courage for her to come forward, argue the Democrats, exposing herself to the further indignity of media scrutiny and death threats. So should we call Ford a "heroine" and "courageous" and a "very fine woman?" If we do, we ignore her iniquitous behavior—*she made a deliberate unsubstantiated accusation of another human being.* Ford's assault does not give her the right to destroy the life of an innocent person.

Attacking a man like Judge Kavanaugh without evidence constitutes a reprehensible act. Ford must assume responsibility for that. If you believe she was telling the truth, that is a subjective opinion and does not change the fact that there is no evidence other than her statement that "he did it." Our system of justice allows no substitute for evidence. The Democrats ask, what message are we sending to assault victims if we confirm Kavanaugh? *What message are we sending about the justice system if we don't confirm him?*

Prof. Ford may have been assaulted by someone, but without evidentiary proof that Judge Kavanaugh was that someone, the accusation should not have made it to the Senate committee. It should have been vetted and put to sleep for lack of evidence. Ford's allegation that "he did it" is not evidence. The accusation has been rebutted by the people she claims were there— including her own friend—and by Kavanaugh's diary. He swears he never attended the party where she was assaulted.

Ford's testimony is rife with holes and inconsistencies. She doesn't remember when it happened, where it happened, or exactly how many were there. The people she says were there all deny it ever happened. Kavanaugh's journal proves he wasn't there. She says she left the house by herself—how did she get home? Did she sprout wings and fly? She claims she won't get on an airplane then admits she has flown everywhere. From beginning to end, her story does not hold up.

Was she lying? Was he lying? It doesn't matter. Did it happen to her or not? That doesn't matter either. What matters is: Can she corroborate her accusation against Kavanaugh? The question for the Senators who will vote on Kavanaugh's confirmation, says Bill O'Reilly, is: "Was there anything you saw or heard that disqualifies Kavanaugh from serving on the Supreme Court?" The objective answer, O'Reilly insists, is no.

I watched Ford deliver her statement. She appears to be a very disturbed woman—52 years old and a psychology professor but sounds like she is 12. Was her story an implanted memory created during her therapy sessions? She spoke from a prepared script that read like a novel. Was she coached on the content of the script? Was she coached to behave like a victim? Who paid for her lawyers? For the polygraph test? She doesn't know! My gut feeling, based on all of the above together with Kavanaugh's thorough testimony, is that I don't believe her. But, as I said, it doesn't matter.

What matters is that Ford is hiding behind her victimization in order to ruin Kavanaugh's life without a single piece of evidence that he is the one who assaulted her 36 years ago. She must be aware of this, unless she is not in her right mind. Call her a heroine? Put her on a pedestal? Not me. I'd sooner put her in prison for bearing false witness.

American Thinker, October 1, 2018

The Corrupt DoJ vs. the People

Let's do a little pretending. You are living in East Germany in 1960. Stasi, the repressive secret police, have arrested you. As you are languishing in prison, the state prosecutor asks you to cough up information that will be damaging to a certain individual that the state wishes to condemn. The prosecutor's demand is backed up with a threat. If you don't compose the incriminating information he seeks, you will spend the next 40 years behind bars and the state will go after your spouse, your children, and your best friend Fido. Everyone you love will be destroyed.

Ah, but you say, "This is America in 2019. That could never happen here. Aren't we lucky to be living in the land of the free and home of the brave?" Well, guess what, Poopsie, this *used to be* the land of the free. Thanks to the politicized justice system that was set in motion more than 20 years ago and reinforced during eight fateful years of the Obama administration, the quaint notion that we benefit from due process has evaporated along with Cinderella's ball gown and fancy coach. A former federal prosecutor by the name of Sidney Powell has blown the whistle. If you watched the January 27th episode of *Life, Liberty and Levin* on the Fox channel, you heard Ms. Powell dispel the illusion that our justice system is fair and impartial.

Powell, author of *Licensed to Lie: Exposing Corruption in the Department of Justice*, described a system consisting of out-of-control prosecutors who will do anything to get a conviction. She accused the Justice Department of a broad range of offenses. Some of those include:

• False charges brought by overzealous prosecutor Andrew Weissmann (Robert Mueller's right-hand-man) in the case against leading accounting firm Arthur Andersen. Although the conviction was subsequently reversed unanimously by the Supreme Court, Andersen was completely destroyed, its 85,000 employees lost their jobs, and the assets of untold investors were wiped out. Weissmann was promoted by the DoJ.

• Destruction of the lives of four Merrill Lynch executives. Before they could appeal their fake convictions, they were sent to prison with the toughest criminals in the country. "They did the worst things they could possibly do to these men," says Powell. The defendants were eventually exonerated on appeal, but it was only after one of them served eight months in solitary confinement.

• Frequent failure by the DoJ to disclose evidence favorable to defendants as required by law.

• Using the phony Steele dossier, the DoJ and FBI unlawfully obtained FISA warrants for the surveillance of the Trump election campaign. The dossier was then used to justify creation of a special counsel to investigate alleged Trump-Russia collusion. After two years, that investigation is nothing more than a witch hunt against Trump supporters.

• Leaking at the top levels of the FBI and DoJ in the midst of criminal investigations.

• Unwillingness of federal judges to discipline the DoJ for its transgressions.

As political commentator Mark Levin has suggested, the Deep State—led by Obama holdovers in the justice system—is using the Mueller investigation as a "silent coup" to unseat President Trump. "Neither Mr. Mueller nor Andrew Weissmann are interested in the truth whatsoever," says Powell. "They're only interested in whatever they can generate to create a criminal offense" against associates of the president. The special counsel's attempt to invalidate a legitimate presidential election is an example of the weaponization of the DoJ in service of political objectives. Mueller coerces witnesses to "compose" evidence capable of bringing down the president. General Michael Flynn, Paul Manafort, Michael Cohen, Jerome Corsi, and others refused to compose and were charged with perjury. Manafort is in solitary confinement after his questionable conviction. There is a name for this: blackmail. Goodbye USA, hello Stasi. If you refuse to lie for us, we will destroy you, your family, and your dog.

The latest target in Mueller's sights is Trump associate Roger Stone. Stone's indictment is described by former US Attorney Joe diGenova as a "vindictive prosecution." "It serves no law enforcement purpose," says diGenova, "It's disgraceful." What is being done to these Trump supporters could just as easily happen to you or me. It's the sort of thing that we would expect in North Korea. If our justice system were functioning as it should, Mueller himself would be charged with blackmail and subornation of perjury—persuading a witness to make a false oath. Instead, the lives of uncooperative witnesses are being destroyed when they are charged with an arbitrary process crime by the special counsel. The FBI has been complicit in Mueller's efforts, as demonstrated by the KGB-style nighttime raids on the homes of Manafort and Stone.

A venal gang of Obama alumni is getting away with the perversion of American justice. What a cast of crooked characters! At the FBI, we have former directors James Comey and Robert Mueller, Andrew McCabe, Peter Strzok, and Lisa Page. At the DoJ: Rod Rosenstein, Andrew Weissmann, Sally

Yates, and Bruce Ohr. From the Obama administration: Hillary Clinton, Loretta Lynch, Eric Holder, Susan Rice, Samantha Power, John Brennan, and Barack Obama himself. The specifics of their illegal activities are described in detail by Greg Jarrett in *The Russia Hoax.*

The civil rights of innocent individuals are being violated for no reason other than their political views. Do you think William Barr, our new attorney general, will do something to stop it? Let's hope he is more effective than his predecessor. Unless the Mueller investigation is terminated and we address the real scandal in our government—corruption at the top levels of the DoJ and FBI—we can kiss the American system of justice goodbye.

American Thinker, February 1, 2019

Chapter 6: The Individual v. Identity Politics

Identity Politics—The Biggest Scam of Our Age

In a period rife with scams, the biggest scam of them all is known as identity politics. According to identity politics and its associated concept of "diversity," people ought to be hired and promoted based on race and gender, not individual characteristics such as hard work and personal sacrifice. The premise of this leftist ideology is that the US is an oppressor nation. Under the banner of diversity, the Left divides Americans between oppressors—heterosexual, Christian, white males—and victimized groups of minorities and women. Because they are victimized, blacks, Hispanics, and women are in need of special protection. "It is the old Marxist wine," says David Horowitz in *Big Agenda*, "and the results are bound to be similar."

The idea that white people are an inherently flawed group of oppressors is absurd on its face. The notion that blacks are victims of a racist society may have been true prior to the 1960s, but this is a half-century after the Civil Rights Movement. "White institutional racism has disappeared from our society," explains author Scott Greer in *No Campus for White Men*. "The oppression of black Americans is over with," African-American author Shelby Steele agreed during an interview with author Mark Levin.

The value system that has made the US successful as a nation is an achievement of white people, especially white men. "The fact that white people are better off is not a privilege," says David Horowitz. "It's earned." White men founded our republic. White men gave their lives to end slavery. White men are largely responsible for the day-to-day commerce that puts food on the table and clothing on our backs. Like it or not, white people and their value system drive the engine that makes this country work. They should not be penalized for their contribution, yet that is the goal of identity politics.

Our country is strong because it is a meritocracy. Merit—being the best—has always been prized in America. Meritocracy and diversity are opposites. Identity politics is based on the eradication of merit. The Left wants success to be based on one's race and gender, not quality and excellence. Identity politics is seducing minorities by offering a chance at the success and affluence that are possible in America but without having to make the effort or personal sacrifices normally needed to obtain them.

The number one reason that minorities have lagged behind whites is an unwillingness to accept white values of hard work, education, and taking responsibility for personal success or failure. As a young man, the only "white privilege" I enjoyed was the knowledge that I could enjoy the American Dream if I earned it. In school, the military, and the world of work, whatever success I achieved was based on my striving for excellence. I studied with diligence, cleaned toilets at night to get through college, met the exacting standards of Marine Corps Officers Candidate School, and always went the extra mile to be the best at whatever profession I practiced. Unfortunately, many blacks and Hispanics are attracted to identity politics because it offers a means of realizing the American Dream without being required to make those personal sacrifices. Where identity politics prevails, you get hired and promoted because of your race and gender and for no other reason.

What an incredible fantasy! You can breeze through life simply because you are African-American or Hispanic or a woman. It is the kind of fantasy that might appeal to children—winning the big prize through the benefit of wizardry. Somebody waves a magic wand and Harry Potter flies around the room. Children have no conception of the sweat that must be invested to be successful in the adult world. And yet here it is being offered on a platter to certain "protected" groups of people.

During the December 2 episode of Fox News' *Life, Liberty and Levin*, author Heather Mac Donald explained that identity politics has taken hold in colleges and universities and is now spreading to the world at large. Companies like Google and Facebook are showing preferences for minorities and women with little regard for qualifications. White men are being discriminated against solely on the basis of skin color and gender. Mac Donald warned about the consequences of this trend. Countries like China and Russia, she said, are meritocracies. If you are a scientist in China, they don't give a damn about your race or gender. If the US falls prey to identity politics, we will never be able to compete on the world stage. Within 20 years, the US could easily turn into a third world country.

Mark Levin raised the question, why do so many affluent whites buy into identity politics? The answer lies in white guilt. Many whites have fallen for the defamatory argument that they do not deserve their "white privilege." So how can identity politics be defeated if even whites are falling for it? The good news is that not all whites or minorities are drinking the Kool-Aid. Half the country voted for Donald Trump because the allure of identity politics is not as strong as the Left would like it to be. We have a choice: vote for conservative politicians or yield the floor to people like Bernie Sanders, Elizabeth Warren, and Kamala Harris. Try to imagine what the US would be like if Bernie or Hillary Clinton had been elected president. As I have argued repeatedly, Donald Trump may go down in history as the man who saved America.

Clash Daily, December 4, 2018

Hollywood's Contempt for Individual Rights

Hollywood celebrities regularly abuse their stardom by engaging in political rhetoric. The latest perpetrator is Frances McDormand, this year's winner of the Best Actress Oscar. She insists that both cast and crew in all movies ought to be composed of at least 50 percent women and minorities. This is her version of diversity, one that I am certain has the stamp of approval from the Left.

How would McDormand remake classic films like *Lawrence of Arabia*, *Patton*, or *The Diary of Anne Frank*...I wonder? Denzel Washington as T.E. Lawrence? Will Smith as General Patton? Oprah Winfrey as Anne Frank? Wait a minute. What about Daniel Day-Lewis as Martin Luther King? Or—if we're really aiming for diversity—Oprah Winfrey as General Patton? That's fine if it accurately represents the director's vision. But what if it doesn't? McDormand doesn't give a damn. She would employ coercion against movie producers who do not adhere to her concept of diversity.

What I object to is not merely the contempt for creative freedom by people who work in a creative profession, but their desire to impose their will by fiat. McDormand envisions a controlling entity—harkening back to the Hays Code censorship of the 1930s—that would impose its dictates upon Hollywood. It is symptomatic of a more pervasive disease: The encroachment of the collective over the rights of the individual.

What makes our society unique in world history is the primacy of individual rights over government intrusion. This is a first in human development. No prior human society enjoyed as its core value the protection of individual rights. Before the Declaration of Independence, the state directed your life from birth to death.

The Founding Fathers, affirming "life, liberty, and the pursuit of happiness," created a republic designed to serve the individual and not the other way around. Respect for the individual is the keystone of our entire value system.

We are at a dangerous moment when all that could be changing. Advocating concepts such as diversity, social justice, and political correctness, the Left is aiming to increase governmental control over every facet of our lives. The platform for this makeover is socialism, where the government takes care of everything. In every case—Soviet Russia, Maoist China, Cuba, Venezuela—socialism has been accompanied by totalitarianism, a dictatorial system demanding complete subservience by the individual to the state.

Way back in 1848, Alexis de Toqueville wrote:

> "Democracy extends the sphere of individual freedom; socialism restricts it. Democracy attaches all possible value to each man; socialism makes each man a mere agent, a mere number. Democracy and socialism have nothing in common but one word: equality. But notice the difference: While democracy seeks equality in liberty, socialism seeks equality in restraint and servitude."

What is the real driving force behind the push for diversity and social justice? Is it a campaign for equality? When Dr. Martin Luther King said, "I have a dream," he was dreaming of equality of opportunity. He was dreaming of a country where people "will not be judged by the color of their skin, but by the content of their character." When the Left advocates diversity, they want equality of outcome. They want people to be judged by their skin color. Character becomes irrelevant as the Left divides Americans into competing groups based on color, ethnicity, and ideology.

With "identity politics," where people take sides based on race, religion, sex, ethnicity, social background, affluence, etc., the American value of respect for the individual is replaced by tribalism. The Huns are at the gates of Rome once again. By empowering groups instead of individuals, says author David Horowitz in *Big Agenda*, the Left is attempting to destroy the inalienable rights of individuals and the right to equal treatment under the law. All of this moralizing and carrying on in the name of diversity, multiculturalism, equality, social justice, and so on, amounts to nothing more than a naked reach for power by "progressive" special interest groups.

Supporters of the social justice movement are not interested in the betterment of mankind. Their objective is social control. Those who identify as "oppressed" want to trade places with their oppressors. This is precisely what happened in the Russian Revolution. Look how it turned out. Stalin murdered more than 20 million people.

The U.S. is a country that values merit over entitlement. A motion picture will succeed or fail on its merits. We can't have a cadre of leftists dictating how films are to be made. If a director wants to remake *Lawrence of Arabia*, don't force him to cast 100 percent women (*Laura of Arabia*) because it conforms to your political ideology. On the other hand, if a director sincerely believes that Oprah will do a great job as Anne Frank, green light it. Well, maybe not.

The important thing to remember is: Allow creative people to be creative and let the individual continue to be the focus of our value system.

Daily Surge, March 7, 2018

Your Choice: Good Grammar or Social Justice?

Here we go again. The gurus of political correctness have struck another blow for doubletalk. American grammar, they say, is racist. At the University of Washington (Tacoma) Writing Center, the people in charge have used "social justice" as an excuse to attack correct grammatical usage. Good grammar, they allege, "may intentionally perpetuate racism or social injustice. We promise to challenge conventional word choices and writing explanations." In an attempt to justify bad grammar, the Center goes on to say:

> *"Linguistic and writing research has shown clearly that there is no inherent 'standard' of English. Language is constantly changing. These two facts make it very difficult to justify placing people in hierarchies or restricting opportunities because of the way people communicate in particular versions of English."*

The school's administration is backing them up. "[The statement] is a great example of how we are striving to act against racism," said the vice chancellor of undergraduate affairs. Mona Chalabi, data editor at *The Guardian US*, agrees:

> *"It doesn't take much to see the power imbalance when it comes to grammar snobbery," Chalabi says. "Grammar snobs are patronizing, pretentious, and just plain wrong. The people pointing out the mistakes are more likely to be older, wealthier, whiter, or just plain academic than the people they're treating with condescension. All too often, it's a way to silence people, and that's particularly offensive when it's someone who might already be struggling to speak up."*

Hey Mona—could it be that the grammar snobs are trying to teach something valuable to these kids who need it very badly?

We have seen this reaction before. A professor at UCLA was disciplined for insisting that his students use the *Chicago Manual of Style*, which is de rigueur for English composition. A sit-in by a group of black students claimed it was offensive and racist. "Asking for better grammar is inflammatory in the school," said an intimidated UCLA teaching assistant. "You have to give an A or you're a racist." In a disgraceful reaction, the school's administration supported the ridiculous claims of the "offended" students. "UCLA's response to the sit-ins was a travesty of justice," wrote author Heather Mac Donald in *City Journal*. "The school sacrificed the reputation of a beloved and respected professor in order to placate a group of ignorant students making a specious charge of racism." The outcome, said Mac Donald, guaranteed that the students "will go through life lodging similar complaints against equally phantom racism and expecting a similarly laudatory response."

This trend on college campuses involves a form of political correctness called *microaggression*, describing insults, intentional or unintentional, by whites against any socially marginalized or "protected" group—blacks, women, Hispanics, gays, Muslims. The offense does not have to be overt. What counts is the subjective reaction of the offended person. In practice, microaggression is used by minorities as a silencing tactic against free speech by censoring anything they don't like as "hate speech." In the Tacoma case, the students apparently were offended by good grammar. This is an effort by minority students to avoid pushing out of their comfort zone. The irony is that without good grammar, they will never be able to get a decent job and so will be stuck in their socioeconomic trap.

Actor and comedian Bill Cosby put his finger on the problem:

> "They're standing on the corner and they can't speak English. I can't even talk the way these people talk: Why

you ain't, where you is, what he drive… Everybody knows it's important to speak English except these knuckleheads. You can't be a doctor with that kind of crap coming out of your mouth. In fact you will never get any kind of job making a decent living. People marched and were hit in the face with rocks to get an education, and now we've got these knuckleheads walking around."

Social justice is scary. It means that minorities don't have to listen to reason because reason—like grammar—is the creation of white people, who are full of crap by virtue of their white privilege. Social justice is opposed to reason. People who demand attention to "diversity" are really against viewpoint diversity, also known as free speech. Diversity means that minorities get control over the system at the expense of the majority, which happens to be white. Unfortunately, as Bill Cosby says, you can't get control over anything if you haven't mastered good grammar.

Ultimately it comes down to a question of standards. Should we seek social justice by lowering the standards to the lowest denominator via affirmative action, or should we require the lowest denominator—in this case, minority students—to meet the higher standard. Lowering standards has given us an educational system that is producing substandard results. So why are thousands of university administrators collaborating with the radical students instead of standing up for higher standards? We need more college administrators like Oklahoma Wesleyan University President Dr. Everett Piper, who told students, "This is not a daycare. This is a university!"

Clash Daily, February 27, 2017

Obama's War on America

During a speech on September 7th to students at the University of Illinois, former President Barack Obama said, "the politics of division and resentment and paranoia has unfortunately found a home in the Republican Party." Once more, the Democrats are attempting to get away with their signature political gambit—blaming their opponents for what they themselves have done.

The most successful accomplishment of the Democrats is what author Mark Levin calls the "balkanization" of society, or what Obama himself referred to as "division and resentment and paranoia." Using their perverted version of "diversity," the Democratic Party—under the leadership of Obama—fomented division and hatred after promising just the opposite. Instead of making everyone feel they are part of a unified American social structure, the Obama presidency played into the leftist strategy of "divide and conquer."

The Democrats use diversity to exploit discontented elements in American society and to invalidate the individual. Mark Levin explains:

> *"It assigns [the individual] a group identity based on race, ethnicity, age, gender, income, etc., to highlight differences within the masses. It then exacerbates old rivalries and disputes or it incites new ones."*

The Left's objective, Levin says, is to "collapse the existing society" by dividing the people against themselves. Rep. Mo Brooks of Alabama explains diversity in terms of vote getting:

> *"It's a part of the Democratic Party's campaign strategy to divide Americans based on skin pigmentation and to try to collect the votes of everybody who is a non-white."*

When you look behind the curtain, diversity is discriminatory. "Diversity in today's America," says Scott Greer in *No Campus for White Men*, "simply means having fewer whites around." The Left, says author Ben Shapiro, wants to portray America as "an incurable mass of bigoted whites." The basis for diversity policy is that certain groups are encouraged to identify themselves as victims of white people. According to African-American author Thomas Sowell, people on the Left like to say, "I am a victim. Therefore, if you do not give in to my demands... you are a hate-filled, evil person."

To progressives, diversity has nothing to do with equality as defined by Dr. Martin Luther King. Instead, they prefer George Orwell's suggestion that (in a totalitarian society) "some animals are more equal than others." The Left's version of diversity means that we must give special privileges to certain protected classes of people so they can acquire control over the system at the expense of the majority. I call this the "tyranny of the minority."

Ironically, where you have obedience to diversity, there is no diversity of thought. People who demand attention to diversity really are against viewpoint diversity, also known as free speech. Diversity means "it is great to look different as long as you think the way I do." Diversity is completely at odds with American values.

So how dare Obama lecture us about the politics of division? After eight years of the Obama presidency, race relations are worse than ever. Obama's comments in case after case—lies and distortions—stoked the fires of racial discord and added to the racial divide. This is ironic because so many Americans—black and white—fully expected that the election of a black president would usher in a period of racial accord. No such luck.

In urging his University of Illinois audience to vote Democratic, Obama had the gall to argue that, "Our democracy depends on it." More hypocrisy from our 44th president. Showing his contempt for the Constitution, Obama did everything he could to expand the power of government at the expense of individual liberty. He strove to "destroy America's essence," says *American Thinker*, "that commitment to liberty that makes her unique in this world."

Donald Trump, in sharp contrast, cherishes the values that Obama holds in contempt. Trump's commitment is to the foundational principles of the Constitution. He rejects minority identity politics. He wants to unify the country in its own self-interest. Trump's objective is to drain the Washington swamp that benefited from Obama's legion of illegal executive orders.

The final straw in Obama's speech was his insistence that we need to restore "honesty and decency" in government. Here are his words:

> *"We do not... use the criminal justice system as a cudgel to punish our political opponents, or to explicitly call on the attorney general to protect members of our own party from prosecution because an election happens to be coming up."*

How can Obama make a statement like that after *his* administration weaponized the IRS against conservative opponents, and after *his* attorney general and FBI conspired to protect Hillary Clinton from the justice she so richly deserved? Well, I guess this is what we should expect from the man who promised, "If you like your plan, you can keep your plan."

American Thinker, September 13, 2018

The *Times* Wants to Drive Identity Politics Down Your Throat

The *1619 Project* is an effort by the *New York Times* allegedly to commemorate the 400th anniversary of slavery's beginning in America. It aims to "reframe the country's history, [understand] 1619 as our true founding, and [place] the consequences of slavery and the contributions of black Americans at the very center of the story we tell ourselves about who we are." In other words, it is propaganda pandering to the new liberal playbook. Slavery was never the central issue in the founding and development of the United States. The experience of slavery was a major factor but not the defining one by any means.

The left-wing *Times* has pushed the false argument that the U.S. is characterized by systemic racism coming from a majority composed of white supremacists. Sorry liberals, the U.S. is not a white supremacist country and blacks are not the center of the American story. Blacks did not found the U.S.—Britain gets the credit for that, as well as the credit for introducing slavery to North America. Slavery was never the focus of U.S. population centers. And what about the prevalence of indentured servitude among the white settlers? Make no mistake about it, the *1619 Project* is an attempt to re-write history as the *Times* kisses the butts of liberals who hate America. It reinforces "identity politics," the aim of which is to divide the country into warring camps based on color and ethnicity.

"The whole project is a lie," said former House Speaker Newt Gingrich. "Certainly if you're an African American, slavery is at the center of what you see at the American experience. But for most Americans, most of the time, there were a lot of other things going on." Gingrich tweeted that the *Times* should make its slogan, "All the Propaganda we want to brainwash you with." Gingrich's conclusion: "*The New York Times'* editor, he basically said, look, we blew it on Russian collusion, didn't work. Now we're going to go to racism, that's our new model. The next two years will be Trump and racism. This is a tragic decline of *The New York Times* into a propaganda paper worthy of Pravda or Izvestia in the Soviet Union."

Echoing Gingrich's point-of-view, conservative commentator Eric Erickson wrote on his blog: "The inmates have taken over the asylum and those inmates are re-writing American history to make everything about race, racism, and slavery." A secret recording has exposed the *Times'* intention to push its "Trump is a racist" angle. Dean Baquet—the first black American to serve as the *Times'* executive editor—told his staff that, in light of the failure of the "Trump and the Russians" campaign, they should focus on Trump's alleged racism. Baquet claimed that race "is going to be a huge part of the American story" and that the *1619 Project* will "teach readers to think a little bit more like that."

American Spectator, a conservative website, was quick to respond: "It's hard to imagine America's former leading newspaper recovering from what its executive editor admitted last week. Baquet says he 'built our newsroom' to cover a story which turns out to have been based on a hoax spread by Democrat Party operatives and used by a corrupt Obama administration to spy on innocent American citizens while attempting to prejudice a presidential election. Baquet now wants to spend the next two years forcing the ashes of that credibility down the collective throat of the American people by spreading non-stop the further hoax of the president's racism."

As a divisive tool, the *1619 Project* is right up there with political correctness and the Green New Deal. If the *Times* gets away with this fiction, what if the next liberal wave is an argument that Latinos are the "very center" of the American story? After all, the Latino population now exceeds that of African Americans. Or will the next version of our history place Native Americans at the center? I can see the *Times* headline: "America's original sin was the genocide of Native Americans."

"If the ownership of the *Times* had any integrity or business sense," *American Spectator* concluded, "they would drop Dean Baquet like a radioactive turd this very day. I can't think of anything more poisonous than a newspaper's executive editor essentially publicly admitting his plan to stoke racial animosity in an effort to influence a presidential election when his charge is to present that publication as an objective deliverer of news. Fulfilling that mission is now impossible."

The bottom line: The *1619 Project* is all about ancient history. None of it contributes to healing the country in the present moment. This preoccupation with race only makes it worse. America may not be perfect, but it is as good as it gets. I am reminded of what Muhammed Ali is reported to have told a Soviet reporter: "To me, the U.S.A. is still the best country in the world." When Ali returned from a trip to Africa, he remarked, "Thank God my granddaddy got on that boat." I wonder what Ali would say about the *1619 Project*.

Reactionary Times, August 21, 2019

Part Three: Politics

"Democracy and socialism have nothing in common but one word: equality. But notice the difference: While democracy seeks equality in liberty, socialism seeks equality in restraint and servitude."
Alexis de Toqueville

Chapter 7: Leftist Ideology

Green New Deal Is Collective Madness in Bloom

Mental illness is a condition that is normally applied to individuals. "She is psychotic." "He is schizophrenic." Under the right conditions, it can also apply to groups. "We know from the sad experience of Nazi Germany or Khmer Rouge Cambodia," says Winslow Meyers at *Commondreams.com*, "that it is possible for whole nations to become mentally ill, with horrendous consequences." Meyers is referring to what psychologists call "social psychosis" or "collective psychosis." We have a new example of collective madness in the "Democratic Socialist" wing of the Democratic Party.

Progressive Democrats have come out of the closet as "Democratic Socialists." Their goal is a utopian society, a reprise of the Soviet Union with an American accent. Every attempt at a socialist utopia has failed. Socialism is a form of big government that rejects the rights of the individual. In every case, it has been accompanied by brutal totalitarianism: Russia under communism, China under Mao, Cuba, and now Venezuela. Tens of millions were murdered under Stalin and Mao. I shudder to think that the U.S. may be heading in the same direction.

The repeated failure of socialism ought to remove it from serious consideration. No such luck. Insanity has been defined as doing the same thing over and over again and expecting a different result. This describes Bernie Sanders, a grumpy old cuss with a Brooklyn accent who has never held a real job but feels entitled to tell the rest of us that we should embrace socialism. Fifty years ago, Sanders would have been laughed off the political stage. What has changed? Leftist professors in our colleges and universities have been indoctrinating young people in the notion that socialism is not merely workable but eminently desirable. As a result, little Bernie Sanders clones are popping up all over the place.

The most charismatic of these Bernie clones is Alexandria Ocasio-Cortez. She sings the same chorus as Bernie but without the crusty old white guy image. AOC is an attractive youthful Latina with incredible chutzpah. According to *Wikipedia*, chutzpah is a Yiddish word meaning "gall, brazen nerve, effrontery, incredible 'guts', presumption plus arrogance." That sums up AOC: arrogant, pathological, with no sense of personal responsibility.

Like her role model Sanders, the fact that AOC has no qualifications does not stop her from telling the rest of us how to behave. A 29-year-old former bartender, she managed to convince New York City voters to send her to Congress despite her ignorance of basic economics and lack of common sense. After one month in Washington, she seems to be calling the shots in the Democratic Party with her demand for a "Green New Deal." Democratic senators Kamala Harris, Elizabeth Warren, and Cory Booker wasted no time buying into it. This is not the first time that a demagogue—a political leader who appeals to the desires and prejudices of voters instead of using rational argument—has been catapulted into power.

The Green New Deal includes: phasing out fossil fuels in ten years, replacing airplanes and cars with high-speed trains, a guaranteed income to people who are "unwilling" to work, healthcare for all, upgrading every building in America for energy efficiency, and an end to cow flatulence (no kidding). Warning that climate change will end the world in 12 years (Al Gore mistakenly predicted the same thing in 2006), AOC has blamed conservatives for suggesting that she wants a massive government takeover. "Obviously, it's not that," she says, "because what we're trying to do is release the investments from the federal government to mobilize those resources across the country." Obviously, it is exactly that—a massive government takeover.

The ironic aspect of the Green New Deal is that it is in service of a monumental hoax known as global warming. The climate hysteria created by Al Gore and friends is based on faulty science. Studies have shown that humans contribute a mere three percent of the CO_2 that is emitted into the atmosphere, hardly enough to cause global warming. In fact, many scientists have recognized the evidence that temperature causes CO_2 to change and not the other way around.

In support of this conclusion is the Global Warming Petition Project, in which 31,000 physicists and physical chemists contend that "there is no convincing scientific evidence that human release of carbon dioxide, methane, or other greenhouse gases is causing or will, in the foreseeable future, cause catastrophic heating of the Earth's atmosphere and disruption of the Earth's climate."

The global warming theory originated in the globalist aspirations of the U.N. "One has to free oneself from the illusion that international climate policy is environmental policy," confessed German economist and UN official Ottmar Edenhofer. "Climate policy has almost nothing to do anymore with environmental protection. The next world climate summit is actually an economy summit during which the distribution of the world's resources will be negotiated." In other words, bureaucrats at the U.N. want to take resources away from us and give them to third world countries. AOC is playing right into their hands.

The Green New Deal would have disastrous economic consequences, including the destruction of the U.S. economy and standard of living, and the loss of millions of jobs. What do we get for this waste of time, money, and effort? Danish environmentalist Bjorn Lomborg has calculated that even if every nation in the world adheres to its climate change commitments by 2030, by the end of this century it will reduce the world's temperatures by a mere 0.048°C or 1/20th of a degree Celsius. Ignorant of the facts, AOC is creating more hysteria—the blind leading the blind.

AOC's proposal is the closest thing we have seen to madness in the political realm. "By the end of the Green New Deal resolution I was laughing so hard I nearly cried," tweeted Kimberley Strassel of the *Wall Street Journal.* "If a bunch of GOPers plotted to forge a fake Democratic bill showing how bonkers the party is, they could not have done a better job."

AOC has plenty of good company in the deranged department: Maxine Waters, Adam Schiff, Chuck Schumer, Nancy Pelosi. The Democratic Party is gradually becoming a refuge for the disturbed and unstable. In the Democratic-controlled media, we have Rachel Maddow, Joe Scarborough, and others who are sliding into incoherence. When you combine the Democratic Socialists with a voting population that swallows their message, it would appear that collective madness is taking hold of our political life. What is the next step in our political evolution? Perhaps a precocious five-year-old will head up the Democratic National Committee. I wouldn't be surprised.

Newsmax, February 8, 2019

The Source of Leftist Intolerance

When I come face-to-face with injustice and falsehood, my blood rises. It just happened with a post I found on *Facebook* (referring to yesterday's shooting attack in the ball park):

> *"Unfortunately the right is already generalizing the blame to left-wing hate and pattern of hostility. Given the level of hatred and hostility the right has routinely expressed toward the left (or anyone who disagrees with them), this is outrageous."*

This is what psychologists call a *projection*, defined as the unconscious transfer of one's own desires or emotions to another person. The writer is projecting irrational leftist hostility onto conservatives. Reality is full of examples that prove the above statement is a flagrant lie. In my new book, *Tyranny of the Minority*, I indict the "vicious intolerance by the Left of any and all conservative opinions." The evidence bears me out.

Consider these recent expressions of hatred and hostility by the Left against the Right: The depiction of Trump's murder at the "Shakespeare in the Park" version of Julius Caesar; Kathy Griffin's display of Trump's bloody head; any utterances about Trump on any given day by Rep. Maxine Waters; Stephen Colbert's disgusting comment about Trump and Putin engaging in a sex act; Robert DeNiro's claim that Trump is a "racist, dog, mutt, bozo, and pig"; Madonna's statement that she wants to blow up the White House; and don't let me forget Sean Hannity's reminder that there have been 12,000 recent tweets calling for the assassination of Trump. And that is just the tip of the iceberg.

Can you remember anything remotely resembling this tirade of filth during the eight years of Obama? Of course you can't, because it didn't happen. In fact, anyone caught criticizing

Obama was immediately labeled as a racist. Clearly the writer of the *Facebook* post was wearing blinders. The policy of the Left is to vilify anyone who disagrees with its ideology. Conservatives, by and large, don't behave like that. As Ben Shapiro says in *Bullies*, conservatives are "generally civil people."

In 1996, Bill Clinton defeated Bob Dole with 49 percent of the popular vote and 379 electoral votes. If you supported Dole, Clinton backers would still talk to you. Not anymore. The simple fact that you are conservative is enough to turn your liberal friends and family against you. It all began with Obama. In 2008, when many acquaintances learned that I was not voting for their hero, they called me a racist. They didn't care about my reasons. To them, no reason was good enough to justify my decision. One of my closest friends told me that I was stupid and has never talked to me again. For the past several months, my Facebook feed has been crawling with nasty, abusive statements charging that all Trump supporters are racists.

What accounts for this intolerant behavior by liberals? Throughout history, some human beings have used their religious beliefs to brutalize non-believers. This approach has wormed its way into the liberal playbook. Progressive liberals behave as though their ideology has been handed down from the mountaintop. Progressivism has morphed into our newest religion. With frightening similarities to Islam, the religion of the Left "is an authoritarian movement that wants total compliance with its dictates," says Daniel Greenfield, Journalism Fellow at the Freedom Center, "with severe punishments for those who disobey."

No longer regarded as merely political contests, elections represent to the Left a duel between good and evil. "Conservatives think liberals are stupid," said author Charles Krauthammer. "Liberals think conservatives are evil." You can tolerate stupidity but you can't countenance evil. "You have to understand progressivism as a kind of religion—specifically a fundamentalist religion," argues *The Federalist*. "In this view of the world, evil takes the form of any barrier to your self-expression." Liberals believe that free speech should not apply to anything they disagree with. "People who violate the progressive code," writes Mark Levin in *Liberty and Tyranny*, "are socially ostracized, sued for discrimination, forced to resign, and driven out of business."

The typical liberal doesn't give a damn about your individual rights or opinions. He only cares about his own point-of-view, which he deems to be infinitely superior. Today's liberal will go on at length about "social justice" and the "common good," but his bottom line is a society that conforms to his ideological aims and his alone. When a belief system is enshrined in a religion, it cannot tolerate criticism. In conformity with this new religion, a Hillary Clinton victory might have placed us closer to a political inquisition in which conservatives would be given the chance to confess and recant. In that scenario, unrepentant conservatives would be deported and replaced by Middle Eastern radicals. Is that so far-fetched? I don't think so. Not when millions of our liberal friends are adopting a holier-than-thou attitude about how to run the country.

Daily Caller, June 16, 2017

Joan of Arc and AOC—History Repeats Itself

In the 15th century, France was losing its war against England. Historian Stephen W. Richey explains how a 17-year-old milkmaid, Joan of Arc, was placed in charge of the French army after it experienced a series of humiliating defeats. "Only a regime in the final straits of desperation," Richey explains, "would pay any heed to an illiterate farm girl who claimed that the voice of God was instructing her to take charge of her country's army and lead it to victory." It was nuts, but in the middle ages they were more inclined to overlook such minor considerations as common sense and evidence.

Fast forward to the 21st century. The Democrats are losing their war against the Republicans. The Dems have not offered up a coherent plan for the country's future. All they have is a series of ad hominem attacks on President Trump. Like the medieval French, they are "in the final straits of desperation." What to do? Voila! Along comes the new Joan of Arc—Alexandria Ocasio-Cortez. Okay, so she isn't a milkmaid from Iowa, but she is an ignorant, 29-year-old bartender from the Bronx. Close enough. The desperate Democrats have imbued AOC with a kind of religious authority that is reminiscent of her French predecessor.

As I explain in *Tyranny of the Minority*, the ideology of the Left has morphed into our newest religion. "You have to understand progressivism as a kind of religion," says *The Federalist*, "specifically, a fundamentalist religion. In this view of the world, evil takes the form of any barrier to your self-expression." Liberals behave as though their socialist ideology has been handed down from the mountaintop. No longer regarded as merely a political contest, elections now represent a duel between good and evil. It makes sense, then, that the Dems would turn to a contemporary incarnation of Joan of Arc, a neophyte with no qualifications, as their savior.

With frightening similarities to Islam, the religion of the Left "is an authoritarian movement that wants total compliance with its dictates," says Daniel Greenfield, Journalism Fellow at the Freedom Center, "with severe punishments for those who disobey." Sure enough, AOC demands total compliance with her Green New Deal and has threatened to punish Democratic colleagues that vote Republican by placing them "on a list." Stalin where are you?

While Joan of Arc was a Christian fanatic, AOC's fanaticism appears to have more in common with Muhammad than Christ. The result is the same. Voters are scared to death that the sky is falling. "People who violate the progressive code," says Mark Levin in *Liberty and Tyranny*, "are socially ostracized, sued for discrimination, forced to resign, and driven out of business."

As we evaluate AOC's Green New Deal, it should be recalled that religious doctrine often disregards common sense and evidence—the evidence, for example, that socialism doesn't work. The repeated failure of socialism ought to remove it from serious consideration. No such luck. Insanity has been defined as doing the same thing over and over again and expecting a different result. Try telling that to Bernie Sanders and AOC. As typical progressive liberals, they envision a socialist utopia that will solve all human problems despite the clear proof that it never solved them before. With their Green New Deal, the Left "substitutes glorious predictions and unachievable promises for knowledge, science, and reason," says Mark Levin in *Ameritopia*, "while laying claim to them all."

Bernie dreams of a world "where poverty is absolutely unnecessary, where international relations are not based on greed, where human beings can own the means of production and work together rather than having to work as semi-slaves to other people who can hire and fire." When you break it down, it amounts to a lot of hot air. The truth is that the GND must not be adopted because it wouldn't work, and if it did, it would destroy the U.S. economy and our entire standard of living. There is no evidence that income redistribution would contribute to anyone's lifestyle, except for the Democratic Party elite that will run the show. Even if we eliminated all fossil fuels, cars, airplanes, cow flatulence, yadda, yadda, the earth's climate would not be altered by one speck of dust.

GND is based on the faulty science of global warming. "A large and growing number of distinguished scientists and engineers," reports the *Wall Street Journal*, "do not agree that drastic actions on global warming are needed." Climate change is a natural phenomenon, says geologist Ian Plimer. "It has been going on for millions of years." Temperature has been constant for 20 years, says Nobel laureate Ivar Giaever. "Climate changes all the time," he adds, "and it's nothing to do with global warming." In other words, there is no problem. Who in their right mind wants a solution to a non-existent problem?

So why is AOC trying to scare the hell out of us with the messianic prediction that, without GND, the world will come to an end in 12 years? The answer is simple. The Dems care about nothing other than raw political power. Their last savior, Hillary Clinton, lost the election. Under Trump's presidency, the economy is a roaring success. Perhaps with a new version of Joan of Arc, the Left can convince enough gullible voters that we should destroy America so the Dems can rule over us. Hallelujah and pass the ammunition!

Clash Daily, March 2, 2019

Why You Should Never Vote Democratic Again

Many Americans vote Democratic because it is a tradition in their families, as it was in mine. The Democratic Party of my childhood espoused values that once were considered American values: the importance of individual rights; freedom of speech; the rule of law; equality of opportunity via free market competition; acceptance of personal responsibility. Remember those? But today's Democratic Party is not the party of your parents and grandparents. The Democrats have abandoned traditional values in favor of a neo-Marxist philosophy. Their values are those of Venezuela and Cuba. Wherever those values have been embraced, we have witnessed economic disaster and personal tragedy on a massive scale.

Today's Democratic Party militates for increased governmental control over every aspect of our lives; limitations on free speech and freedom of the press; replacement of capitalism with socialism, and meritocracy with race-based criteria; a reduction of American power and influence; and a dysfunctional version of social justice. All of these items were part of Obama's platform. Obama hates America. If Hillary Clinton had been elected, we would be suffering under a continuation of Obama's destructive agenda.

The lies invented by Democrats suggest that the election of Obama as the first African-American president justified all of his anti-American policies and rampant incompetence. This in itself is a racist notion. The Democrat's conception of "social justice" may sound like a good idea, but in reality it is designed to divide the country into warring factions based on the idea that minority groups are oppressed by "racist white America." White people are targeted as the enemy. Democrats have endorsed attempts to decrease the percentage of the population that is white, largely by inviting more and more illegal immigrants who presumably will vote Democratic.

Here, then, is a summary of the reasons why you should never vote Democratic again. If you are white, the Democrats are throwing white Americans under the bus by accusing them of premeditated systemic racial oppression of minorities. Unless you are into self-hate, don't vote for the party that is actively working to replace you. This, by the way, is no exaggeration. You won't hear much about it in the media because they are in the pocket of the Democratic Party.

If you are non-white, there are two reasons not to vote for Democrats. First, the Democratic Party has devoted the last 50 years to destroying the meaning of the Civil Rights Act of 1964, which aimed for equality of opportunity by outlawing discrimination on the basis of race, religion, color, sex, and national origin. People were to be judged not by the color of their skin, but by the quality of their character. When the Democrats advocate diversity, they want people to be judged by the color of their skin. In a "multicultural" Democratic world, character becomes irrelevant as the Democrats divide Americans into competing groups based on color and ethnicity. The potential damage to race relations is incalculable.

Second, the welfare state advocated and implemented by Democrats has trapped "people of color" in its hateful web. "The belief that people are entitled to what others have produced," said economist Thomas Sowell, "is at the heart of the social degeneration that can be traced back to the 1960s." The breakdown of the black family, teenage pregnancies, and increased crime in black communities can all be traced back to the welfare state, said Sowell.

In other words, the social vision of the Democratic Party has been the enemy of minorities. The idea that the Democratic Party is the working man's party is a fiction. "Far from being the party of the people, Democrats represent America's social and cultural elites," said author David Horowitz. "How is it possible that Democrats and progressives can pose as defenders of minorities, the middle class, and the poor? Democratic policies have devastated all three."

For those of you who are white, black, brown, yellow, or orange, bear in mind that the Democrats are trying to take away your right to free speech, guaranteed by the First Amendment. If the Democratic Party has its way, you won't be able to fart without government approval. A landmark California bill that would have destroyed the First Amendment by making it illegal to engage in climate change dissent was supported by then-California Attorney General Kamala Harris, the very same Senator Harris who is being touted as a possible Democratic presidential candidate. The fact that someone who has actively campaigned against freedom of speech is acceptable to the Democratic Party is reason enough to send us all rushing into the arms of the Republicans.

If the Democratic Party succeeds in its campaign to redistribute income, we will have a country in which half the population is supported by the other half. The productive half that is doing the supporting will throw up their hands in disgust. The incentive to achieve will disappear, as it has in parts of Europe. "To hell with this," entrepreneurs will declare. "I'm tired of being a slave to people who refuse to be responsible for themselves." And do you know what they will do? They will pack up and leave. It is happening right now in France and other European countries as socialist governments ratchet up the tax rates in order to pay for their rapacious nanny states.

When the productive segment of our population moves to Argentina, New Zealand, and Singapore, what will we become? Venezuela.

Media Equalizer, June 8, 2018

Will the Real Fascist Please Stand Up—The Left's Assault on Individual Rights

It is five o'clock in the morning and I am suffering from jetlag. Instead of getting the sleep I sorely need, my mind keeps replaying an interview that I watched on *Fox News*.

Judge Jeanine Pirro was being accosted by a cantankerous, middle-aged black man who described himself as a communist. He was expressing his utter disdain for the election of Donald Trump. This man did not vote for the president-elect because Trump, he says, is a fascist. Since he didn't vote for Trump, this man doesn't feel he is required to accept the results of the election...and he doesn't want you to accept it either. In fact, he wants you to act out your disapproval by doing everything you can to protest Trump and the fascism he represents.

"Are you an anarchist?" Pirro asked, getting right at the core of the matter as she always does. You could tell that she hit him where it hurt. Instead of answering the question, the man went from the ridiculous to the ultra-absurd, comparing Trump to Hitler. This interview is a perfect example of how the left attempts to project its own fascistic tendencies onto the right.

The way it works in this republic is, we have an election and the winner is the president for the next four years. When Obama was elected in 2008, I didn't like it but the voters had spoken and I knew I would have a chance to change it in 2012. Progressives don't feel they have to abide by this basic concept. They believe that they are wiser than the rest of us. Therefore they are entitled to subvert the entire process. That sounds to me like fascism.

Coincidentally, I just happen to be reading a 1944 book entitled *The Road to Serfdom* by F.A. Hayek, a man whose ideas were way ahead of his time. Hayek places fascists and socialists at one end of the political spectrum, and respect for the rights of the individual at the other end. His thesis is that a collectivist ideology—socialism, communism, fascism—will always lead to totalitarianism and the obliteration of individual rights. He believes that "the force which built our civilization" is the acknowledgment of the rights of the individual. "Freedom from coercion, freedom from the arbitrary power of other men." This originally was a liberal concept, Hayek explains, but today's liberals have a different approach to social problems. "The change," he says, "amounts to a complete reversal...an entire abandonment of the individualist tradition which has created Western civilization."

Judge Pirro's interview subject is a classic contemporary liberal "progressive." He doesn't give a damn about your individual rights. He only cares about his own point-of-view, which he deems to be infinitely superior. "Democracy and socialism have nothing in common but one word: equality," said Alexis de Tocqueville in 1848. "But notice the difference: while democracy seeks equality in liberty, socialism seeks equality in restraint and servitude." Ironically, the enemy of Pirro's interviewee is the older version of liberal who cared about liberty and individual rights. Today's liberal will go on at length about "social justice" and the "common good," but his bottom line is a society that conforms to his ideological aims and his alone.

And that is why it is 5:00AM and I can't sleep. This aggravating man on Judge Pirro's TV show represents a palpable danger to our republic because he seeks to destroy the very assumptions that make this country possible. He calls Trump a fascist, but in reality he is the fascist. I believe in the rights of the individual and the rule of law, the opposite of anarchy. My perception is that Donald Trump shares my belief system. Trump's political ideology is the diametrical opposite of fascism.

Under the ideological leadership of Obama and his friends from Chicago, the Democratic Party has been waging war on individual freedoms, especially the freedom of speech. They have attempted to demonize and prosecute anyone who denies the left's global warming agenda, or who is guilty of "anti-Muslim rhetoric," or who advocates a stronger military. The Obama presidency has encouraged left-wing extremists—like Pirro's guest—to come out of the woodwork. I take comfort that, under President Trump, the ideological balance will swing back to a semblance of sanity—by which I mean respect for individual rights and the rule of law.

Okay, now I can get some sleep.

Daily Surge, January 10, 2017

Never Ride in an Elevator with an Angry Leftist

Violent behavior has become one of the hallmarks of the American Left. On the one hand, we have the Nazi-like Antifa mobs that attack conservatives with sticks and chains, and on the other, Rep. Maxine Waters, who attacks them with her mouth—exhorting her followers to harass Trump supporters wherever they can find them. Leftist protestors appear to be suffering from two pathological behavior patterns: freedom to disobey laws they don't like, and refusal to assume responsibility for the consequences of their actions.

The Left wants a bigger federal government that will run every aspect of our lives. The existence of violent protestors is used to justify increased government intervention, including martial law. This would be a means to the Left's ideological objective: the transformation of America into an authoritarian socialist nation run by unaccountable bureaucrats.

A classic example of leftist violence raised its ugly head last week in the middle of the Brett Kavanaugh Supreme Court confirmation hearings. After voting in favor of confirmation, Sen. Jeff Flake of Arizona was accosted in an elevator by two angry women who managed to get past security. As the women prevented the elevator from moving, one of them cornered Flake. She screamed and wildly gesticulated at the discomfited senator:

> *"Don't look away from me! Look at me and tell me it doesn't matter what happened to me.* [She claimed that she was sexually assaulted.] *What you are doing is allowing someone who actually violated a woman to sit on the Supreme Court. You're telling all women that they don't matter. This is not tolerable!"*

The outburst continued for over a minute as Sen. Flake cowered against the sides of the elevator. It seemed more like an hour.

The angry protestor was Ana Maria Archila, Co-Executive Director of the Center for Popular Democracy, a liberal advocacy group. Archila appears to be a disciple of Maxine Waters. Neither Archila nor Waters believes in due process. Archila has convicted Kavanaugh of assaulting Christine Blasey Ford despite the complete absence of evidence, and she wants Flake to do the same. Kavanaugh, who denies Ford's accusation, is being held accountable by Archila for all the women who have ever been assaulted. He is guilty until proven innocent. Watching Archila on that elevator sends a chill up and down my spine.

Archila's brand of out-of-control anger is the modus operandi of the Left. In typical leftist fashion, she does not tolerate the free expression of contrary viewpoints. When confronted by those viewpoints, the Left will attempt to silence them by shouting them down or by resorting to violence. What Archila did amounts to an assault upon a member of the US Senate yet no one attempted to stop her. On the contrary, Archila became a media darling when she was interviewed by Anderson Cooper on CNN.

Archila's supporters falsely insist that her protest was peaceful. Some even call her the new Rosa Parks. Given the intensity of the physical and vocal threat, to call it anything other than violent is outrageous. Why was Archila not arrested for assault? Why isn't Maxine Waters in jail for inciting violence? After the elevator incident, Sen. Flake changed his tune and requested a new FBI investigation of Judge Kavanaugh. Such capitulation in the face of intimidation will only encourage more violent behavior by Archila and her ideological comrades.

A similar pattern of leftist intimidation has emerged in Europe. The European public finally figured out what the Left is doing and a defense is being mounted. It may be too late for them. It's time we did the same before it is too late for us. If leftist intimidation goes unchallenged, the United States in 2038 will be unrecognizable to most of us who are alive today. It will be familiar to those who have lived in Cuba, Venezuela, or North Korea. America, once home of the brave and land of the free, will be a Stalinist state with power going to a few—a tyranny of the minority.

Clash Daily, October 1, 2018

The Self-Destruction of the Democratic Party

When Donald Trump assumed the office of president in 2017, his attempt to do the job for which he was elected met with vicious opposition from every quarter. Although we had a Republican president and a Republican Congress, the government that Trump inherited from his predecessor seemed to be out of control. Who, then, was actually running the country?

Provable crimes by Hillary Clinton and other Democratic members of the Obama administration were brushed off by the Justice Department. Instead, the Mueller investigation—which seems to have a life of its own—moved to invalidate the results of the presidential election. Acting Attorney General Sally Yates refused to enforce Trump's immigration ban. The ruling of one rogue federal district judge was sufficient to stop the executive branch from functioning for a year and a half. Congressional committees were told to pound sand when they demanded accountability from the bureaucracy in the FBI and Justice Department.

And so I ask this question once again: *Who runs the country?* Is it run by the president? Is it run by the unelected bureaucrats of the Deep State? Is it run by Nancy Pelosi? The answer can be found by looking at the three main supports upon which our government rests: the rule of law, separation of powers, and checks and balances. When all of these pillars are respected, there is no question about *who* is running the country. The government runs itself as it was designed to do, through relatively smooth coordination of its constituent elements.

Thanks to one man and his disciples, the smooth coordination came to a halt in 2009. That man, Barack Hussein Obama, was the first sitting president to attempt the disembowelment of the

United States. He was telling the truth when he said he wanted to "fundamentally transform America." Obama hates America. His objective as president was to undermine the very Constitution he swore to defend. In order to subvert the legislative and judicial branches, he issued a legion of illegal executive orders and appointed thousands of bureaucrats and federal judges who would support his anti-American policies. As we are discovering, civil servants appointed by Obama make their own rules. Obama's activist judges behave as lawmakers rather than law interpreters.

Donald Trump is attempting to move the train back onto the tracks. By replacing Obama bureaucrats and appointing constitutionalists—not judicial activists—to the Supreme Court, he is ensuring that the system runs as it was intended. The Democrats complain that Trump wants to pack the court with conservatives. Their argument misses the point entirely. The Supreme Court was not created to make laws. That is the job of Congress. A court of judicial activists, whether conservative or liberal, will undermine the republic. The only way to save the court and the country is with the appointment of jurists who are faithful to the Constitution, which, by the way, is worth defending. We should be grateful that Trump understands this.

Unfortunately, the new Democratic Party thinks the Constitution is a dirty word. Democrats Nancy Pelosi, Chuck Schumer, Tom Perez, Bernie Sanders, Maxine Waters, and Alexandria Ocasio-Cortez want borders open to all comers, disregard for the rule of law when it suits their agenda, restrictions on free speech, free healthcare for all, and the elimination of free markets. By pushing distorted versions of diversity, social justice, and political correctness, the Democrats want increased governmental control over every facet of our lives.

The platform for this makeover is socialism, where the government takes care of everything. "Every single one of [Obama's] initiatives," says *American Thinker*, was "directed at increasing government control in every area, with a corresponding decrease in individual liberty." In each and every case—Soviet Russia, Maoist China, Cuba, Venezuela—socialism has been accompanied by totalitarianism, a dictatorial system demanding complete subservience to the state.

When will the "progressive" voices of the Democratic Party be moderated by the voice of reason? At the moment, it doesn't look promising. Democrats come across as foul-mouthed and violent. Maxine Waters urges Democrats to follow Republicans into restaurants in order to harass them. Antifa protestors are brown shirts in all but name. Republican congressmen (e.g., Steve Scalise) are valid target practice for disgruntled Democrats with live ammunition. As the party of victimization, the Democrats vilify white Americans by accusing them of oppressing everybody else.

The time has come for a complete reformation of the Democratic Party. If they continue in this direction, Democrats will lose elections in all but the most left-wing electoral districts. The Democratic Party will become irrelevant. This is not healthy for a country that depends on a multi-party system.

Eagle Rising, July 21, 2018

A Guaranteed Income is the Guarantor of Social Collapse

A generous Chicago alderman has proposed giving people a guaranteed income of $500 per month. A would-be Democratic presidential candidate wants to up the monthly stipend to $1,000. "The growth of the welfare state," says CNN, "is turning us into a land where many expect, and see no stigma attached to, drawing regular financial support from the federal government." Even some conservatives have succumbed to the concept of guaranteed income, reports *Investor's Business Daily*. They dream of "eliminating the dozens of welfare programs at the federal, state and city levels and replacing them with one big check." Is it a good idea?

Democrats Barack Obama, Bernie Sanders, and Alexandria Ocasio-Cortez think it's a great idea, as do entrepreneurs Elon Musk and Mark Zuckerberg. How would they pay for it? By redistributing income, naturally. First, tax the rich. Then burden corporations with a value-added tax as they do in Europe. Proponents conveniently overlook the fact that Europe is reeling under the burden of the Nanny State. "The simplest way in which the advanced welfare state will lose attractiveness," says Charles Murray, author of *Coming Apart*, "is the looming bankruptcy of the European welfare states."

Unfortunately, many Americans have bought into the belief that poverty can be eliminated by throwing money at it. What else could account for the popularity of Sanders and Ocasio-Cortez? There is no doubt about it—people enjoy receiving free stuff. To believe this way is to fall for the leftist hoax that the answer to all our problems is bigger government enforcing a comprehensive redistribution of resources.

Forget about the fiscal irresponsibility of the guaranteed income plan. The purely economic drawbacks of the welfare system are dwarfed by the resulting cultural damage. Welfare entitlement is at odds with the American values known as hard work and accepting responsibility. The Nanny State makes people lazy. Europe has witnessed the replacement of the traditional continental work ethic with a sense of entitlement, says *Brussels Journal*, "while the high taxation and the passivity bred by the system [have] eroded initiative and the will to take risks."

Under our culture of dependency, welfare recipients lose the work habits and job skills that would otherwise make them independent. Poverty is transferred from generation to generation with no hope in sight. "A significant and growing portion of the American population," says Charles Murray, "is losing the virtues required to be functioning members of a free society."

The primary fallacy of welfare payments and income redistribution is that they do nothing to end the pattern of poverty. Robbing Peter to pay Paul does no good without rehabilitating Paul. I like the old saw that if you give a man a fish you feed him for a day but if you teach him how to fish you feed him for a lifetime. Our current system of welfare entitlements is the equivalent of giving a man a fish. It benefits no one but the charter members of the Victimization Industry, people like Jesse Jackson and Al Sharpton.

When people receive free basics—food, shelter, and the like—from the government, it precludes the possibility of personal responsibility. In terms of survival, Murray argues that accepting responsibility is the most important value. Without it, he says, life has no meaning. The challenges of life are diminished. People lose the incentive to live their lives and they turn into robots. "All of the good things in life," says Murray, "require freedom to act coupled with responsibility for the consequences of those actions... The only way to earn anything is to achieve it in the face of the possibility of failing." With any accomplishment in life, he concludes, "responsibility for the desired outcome is inseparable from the satisfaction."

How do we provide support for low-income Americans while helping them to be responsible for their actions? Offering a guaranteed income can only make the situation worse. We will never put an end to poverty without replacing the "give them free stuff" welfare mentality with programs that prepare the recipients for self-sufficiency. President Trump understands this. He has signed an executive order that will strengthen work requirements for public assistance. "Part of President Trump's effort to create a booming American economy," says the White House, "includes moving Americans from welfare to work" and helping them "reclaim their independence." It is about time.

Eagle Rising, July 30, 2018

Bernie Sanders' Big Lie About Government-Run Healthcare

Sen. Bernie Sanders has repeatedly claimed that the US is the only country in the world that does not provide access to healthcare for all its citizens. "If every major country on earth can guarantee healthcare to all," Sanders said, "and achieve better health outcomes, while spending substantially less per capita than we do, it is absurd for anyone to suggest that the United States cannot do the same."

Sanders, an admitted socialist, goes on to argue that, "Healthcare must be recognized as a right, not a privilege. Every man, woman and child in our country should be able to access the health care they need regardless of their income. The only long-term solution to America's health care crisis is a single-payer national health care program."

Sounds persuasive, doesn't it? Except for one thing—it is a complete lie! First, the assertion that all US citizens do not have access to healthcare is ridiculous. "Everybody and anybody," says author Mark Levin, "gets access to the same treatment just by walking into the emergency room." We have access to more and better healthcare than any country in the world. And that is true regardless of your income.

Second, to suggest that the rest of the world "achieves better health outcomes" runs counter to reality. See what kind of outcome you get in the UK, for example, where healthcare is a right. "Their healthcare system sucks," says Levin. "They can't get the kind of care they need in a timely fashion. Everybody has yellow teeth because dental care is a right." Operations are hard to schedule and often are cancelled. There is a lack of access to innovative treatments. There is a shortage of beds. The demand cannot be met. Yes, healthcare is a right, but the quality of that healthcare is abysmal.

When people want the best healthcare, they come to the US for a very good reason: nowhere on the planet do people have a better chance of survival than in America. We have the best doctors and the best hospitals. "Every major country in Europe sucks," says Levin. "Their heathcare system sucks. We shouldn't seek to copy Europe. Europe should seek to copy us."

And what about Bernie's idea of a single-payer national healthcare program? With the exception of the military, everything government touches is a disaster. Look at what happened to the Veterans Administration. "Centralized government cannot manage a complex system," observes Levin. "They can't even manage the Obamacare website." According to *Forbes Magazine*, "Single-payer systems have failed everywhere they've been implemented, from the United Kingdom to Canada. Americans who fall for single-payer's promise of 'universal health coverage' at lower cost will instead find themselves facing long waits for subpar care."

What makes our healthcare system work is the availability of choices. In Europe, you have to accept the lousy service offered by their national healthcare systems. Americans have more choices than any country on earth. If the government takes charge of your health, you will no longer decide what treatment you receive—government bean counters will make that decision. This will be especially hurtful for seniors and others who could be denied costly procedures.

Offering a choice of services is the way we maintain higher healthcare standards. Our high standards will disappear the moment government decides that healthcare is a right. Government mismanagement will destroy all the good features of the current system. If doctors are forced to work for the government, the incentive to study medicine will disappear and we can expect an immediate downgrade in quality of care.

Finally, I haven't even mentioned the cost of government-run healthcare. Sally Pipes, president of Pacific Research Institute, suspects that much of the support for a single-payer system is because politicians (such as Alexandria Ocasio-Cortez) run on "pie-in-the-sky" promises of eliminating premiums, copays, and deductibles while giving few details about how to pay for such a plan. "People support single payer when you ask them if they'd like a system that eliminates everything they don't like about the current system," says Pipes, "but when you ask them if they want to pay more taxes that support goes down."

"Single-payer will bankrupt our country," warned President Trump, "because it's more than we take in, for just health care." Sanders estimates his program will cost $1.38 trillion per year. The Urban Institute says no, it will cost $2.5 trillion a year. The Committee for a Responsible Federal Budget estimates the cost at $2.8 trillion per year. The libertarian Mercator Center puts the figure at $3.26 trillion. "Even doubling all federal individual and corporate income taxes wouldn't cover this cost," says House Speaker Paul Ryan. "It is just absurd."

That's right, Bernie, turning control over healthcare to the government is the worst idea ever invented. Yet how many people voted for Bernie in the presidential election? We are still a gullible electorate. Perhaps when Americans comprehend the failure that is European healthcare, they will finally get the message.

Clash Daily, November 30, 2018

Elizabeth Warren: The Political Version of Charles Manson

John F. Kennedy's most famous line was, "Ask not what your country can do for you—ask what you can do for your country." In 1960, it sounded sweet and inoffensive. The enormous sacrifices made during World War II were still echoing in the air. We liked the idea of pitching in. Sixty years later, we are discovering what Kennedy really meant and what the Democrats have had in mind the entire time: The individual exists to serve the state, not the other way around. What can you do for your country? EVERYTHING.

Hold it. Didn't the Founding Fathers invent the United States as protection against this very notion? What makes America unique in world history is the insistence on limited government: the primacy of the individual over the state. Hitler. Mussolini. Stalin. Mao. Castro. At great cost in human life, their regimes coerced the individual to serve the state. We have been fortunate to live in a nation the very purpose of which is to prevent a Hitler or Castro from taking over. Let's be thankful for this.

Enter Elizabeth Warren. Hiding behind a distorted version of "compassion," she wants to provide free healthcare for everyone at a cost of only $52 trillion. What a bargain. After all, she argues that healthcare is a right. Bear in mind that the annual federal budget is $4 trillion. Where does Warren hope to find the money to pay for her largesse? Tax the very rich, naturally.

The ultra-rich are a small minority, small enough to be taken advantage of by a greedy majority. Warren is betting that the majority will say, "Great idea, let's tax those rich bastards." Make them pay their "fair share." Obama paved the way for scalping the affluent when he said, "You didn't build that." He was talking about Bill Gates and Larry Ellison and Warren Buffett. How dare they hoard all the money that really belongs to you and me? This is how socialists think.

Okay, so we take most of their money—excuse me, our money. What if a handful of billionaire fortunes is insufficient to feed the monster? Then we take it down a peg and tax the hell out of millionaires. You see where this is going? Eventually you wind up over-taxing everybody in order to feed the rapacious ship of state. Warren believes that all of America's resources—everything you and I have worked for—belong to the federal government. So what if two million people lose their jobs, as she herself predicts. For Warren, the state takes precedence over the individual. If people have to suffer in order to satisfy Warren's compassionate agenda, too damn bad. When you remove the curtain, Warren is the new incarnation of Stalin, the political version of Charles Manson, with a gargantuan appetite in search of control over the masses.

We need to understand that it doesn't stop with healthcare. The aim of "Democratic Socialists" like Warren and Bernie Sanders is a bloated government in Washington run by a cadre of unelected, unaccountable bureaucrats and overseen by a tiny elite for whom the rules do not apply. It is the Soviet Union all over again. Obama pushed Obamacare because he knew that when he had control over the healthcare system, it would be a matter of time before the government controlled everything. Warren is Obama on steroids. Her policies are a smokescreen for enforcing the dystopian reality portrayed by George Orwell in *1984*. If you haven't read it, get a copy. It describes the world according to Warren.

The Democratic Socialists object to Donald Trump's presidency because he was installed by the ignorant electorate contrary to the wishes of the Deep State. In other words, they don't believe in elections. Warren and Sanders and Obama can live in mansions with servants—just as Stalin did—while the rest of us suffer from the collapse of our economic system, a system that has provided more for the masses than any other in history. And collapse it will as the Democratic Socialists deconstruct capitalism. They have allies in the United Nations and the European Union, both of which are run by unelected bureaucrats who want to destroy national sovereignty. The bureaucrats at the UN have admitted that their campaign to combat global warming is really an all-out effort to redistribute resources on a global scale.

The irony is that we have come full circle from the McCarthyism of the 1950s. Warren's ideas would have landed her in jail in 1954. What happened? The American Left has succeeded in infiltrating the Democratic Party, academia, the media, and Hollywood. Today's college students are told that socialism will work in the US despite the fact that it has failed everywhere else. So what can we do about it? Those of us who still believe in limited government and the capitalist system can fight for our beliefs. We can reject the fake news media, we can reject political correctness, we can stop going to see propagandistic Hollywood films, and we can reeducate the young to appreciate political realities.

Warren is dangerous. If she succeeds in taking over the Democratic Party, the ballot box choice will be clear: a federal republic or a totalitarian socialist state. Give thanks for Trump. Whether or not you like his bombastic style, what counts is that he supports American values: free speech, limited government, checks and balances, due process and the rule of law, equality of opportunity via free market competition, private property, acceptance of personal responsibility. The Left wants to do away with all of it. What about you? What do you support? Now is the time to stand up for what you believe.

Reactionary Times, November 10, 2019

Chapter 8: Racial Politics

Calling Someone Racist Without Proof is Part of the Liberal Playbook

My 83-year-old buddy plays handball twice a week with three other octogenarians. Their YMCA has two handball courts, one of which is preferred because the lighting is better. Yesterday, the senior athletes arrived at the Y only to discover four black women doing their stretching workout on the good handball court. The men, all of whom are white, politely asked the women if they wouldn't mind doing their exercises on the other court so the men could play ball on the court with decent lighting. The women said okay and moved to the other court.

Five minutes later, a member of the YMCA staff informed the handball players that they would have to relinquish their court to the women. Then the staff member lowered the boom. The women claimed the men had used the N word. Horror of horrors! Send in the Marines.

The men categorically denied the charge. It didn't matter. The staff member refused to accept the men's denial. The mere accusation by four lying women was sufficient to establish that the dreaded N word had been used. The women were not challenged because calling someone a racist without proof is part of the liberal playbook. Welcome to the Left's new rule for establishing culpability: A mere allegation of wrongdoing is sufficient to convict. Say goodbye to the bulwark of our legal system. You are guilty until proven innocent.

The same rule—the poison of unsubstantiated allegations—was invoked last week in another racially charged situation. The President of the United States was accused by Democratic Sen. Dick Durbin of suggesting that the U.S. should stop accepting immigrants from "shithole countries." Trump is alleged to have said, "Why are we having all these people from shithole countries come here?" According to Durbin, Trump advocated that the U.S. should be taking more immigrants from "countries such as Norway" instead of "shithole" countries like Haiti, El Salvador, and several nations in Africa. His comments allegedly occurred off the record in a meeting between the president and a group of senators. Sen. Durbin called the comments "hate filled, vile, and racist." Durbin, by the way, has a history of making up statements from private White House meetings.

The president issued a denial. "This was not the language used," Trump said in one of his famous tweets. Sens. David Perdue and Tom Cotton, who attended the meeting, backed up Trump's denial by issuing this statement: "In regards to Senator Durbin's accusation, we do not recall the president saying these comments." Despite the president's denial and the concurrence of two senators, the accusation was enough to establish guilt. The mainstream media went absolutely bat crazy with an avalanche of stories accusing Trump of racism because of his "highly incendiary comments."

CNN mouthpieces Anderson Cooper, Don Lemon, Jim Acosta, and Jeffrey Toobin agreed that the alleged outburst proved Trump is a racist. Cooper said on his evening program that the president "is tired of so many black people coming into this country." Trump "seems to harbor racist feelings about people of color, from other parts of the world," said Acosta. "It just shows that, you know, the president has racist views," Toobin said. "I mean, you know, how long do we have to dance around that issue?"

How long do we have to dance around the fake media? The multitude of attacks on the president emanated from an unsubstantiated claim from a single dubious source. Even former Democratic President Jimmy Carter expressed his disgust with the media's eagerness to accept unproven allegations. "I think the media have been harder on Trump than any other president certainly that I've known about," Carter said. "I think they feel free to claim that Trump is mentally deranged and everything else without hesitation." Carter was referring to more unsubstantiated allegations, in this case involving charges that Trump is mentally unfit to be president. Those charges were clearly debunked by the results of Trump's latest physical that included a positive assessment of his cognitive abilities.

The most virulent example of "guilty until proven innocent" has raised its ugly head in the current "me-too" hysteria. Although many of the accusations of sexual misconduct against high-profile men are provable, many are derived from unsubstantiated claims. The reputations and careers of successful men are being destroyed without a shred of evidence. A noteworthy example is the case against Fox News star Bill O'Reilly. O'Reilly was fired last year from his $25 million job after a series of accusations of sexual harassment. None of the allegations against O'Reilly has been proven. He has denied the truth of all charges.

One accusation was from an angry black woman who said O'Reilly called her "hot chocolate." This presumably was a reference to her race. As in the case of the octogenarian handball players, introducing the race card only makes O'Reilly look worse in the eyes of a public that has been trained to respond emotionally to specific cues relating to "social justice." Should a respected man's career be destroyed because he called a woman "hot chocolate?" It really seems ridiculous and yet we have reached a place in our social history where witch hunts are a regular feature and public figures can be brought down by malicious rumors.

What are we supposed to do to safeguard the legal protection afforded by "innocent until proven guilty?" So long as the Left and its media collaborators refuse to defend this principle, we are in big trouble.

LifeZette, January 22, 2018

Our Kids Are Being Taught They're Flawed If They're White

The American Left has morphed into our newest religion. With frightening similarities to Islam, the religion of the Left "is an authoritarian movement that wants total compliance with its dictates," says Daniel Greenfield, Journalism Fellow at the Freedom Center, "with severe punishments for those who disobey." In my new book, *Tyranny of the Minority*, I warn that, "a Hillary Clinton victory might have placed us closer to a political inquisition in which conservatives would be given the chance to confess and recant. In that scenario, unrepentant conservatives would be deported."

Is that so far-fetched? I don't think so. An inquisition aimed at white people is already underway. The January 5, 2018, *Tucker Carlson Show* reported that eighth-graders in West Bend, Wisconsin, were given "a privilege test that identified them for being white or rich or having an intact family." This is common, said Carlson, in schools across the country. School officials in West Bend argued that privilege education is important to "enable the students to succeed in their careers." The officials failed to explain how shaming kids who are 12 and 13 years old will constitute a career booster. "For a lot of children," said one parent, "they don't even understand what most of it means." "If I walked up to a 13-year-old on the street and started asking these questions I'd be put in the back of a squad car," said another parent.

Tucker Carlson challenged the idea that all people of one race are empowered and all people of another race are not. Calling the privilege test "cruel," he said that it shames some kids as being "bad" for things they can't control. "How is this compassionate," Tucker asked, "to single out little kids to make them feel bad about their race or their family situation? Why would they do this to children?" Tucker's question was answered by his guest, a liberal psychologist. It is difficult to teach history, she alleged, without talking about privilege. People must recognize what kind of privilege they have in society, she explained, "perhaps white, perhaps male." Positions of privilege "when they are abused can lead to horrible crimes committed to [sic] humanity." Students must be taught to admit their privilege and not to "abuse" it as "they move forward in their lives. Otherwise we are going to raise little boys who end up becoming producers and executives at large movie studios who end up committing crimes against women like rape."

If 12-year-olds don't confess their privilege, they will all grow up to be sexual predators? She is admitting that the latest rash of sexual abuse allegations is part of the campaign to demonize all white males. The school in West Bend is brainwashing adolescent children to confess that they are flawed if they happen to be white and male. If this is not an inquisition, what is? The privilege test is a manifestation of the Left's attempt to promote its racist/sexist concepts of "white privilege" and "toxic masculinity." It is a species of identity politics described by Scott Greer in *No Campus for White Men* as "bordering on an outright hatred for white people, especially white men." "The Left," says author Ben Shapiro, "wants to portray America as 'an incurable mass of bigoted whites.'"

One of the most popular forms of anti-white discrimination is the indoctrination training forced by many colleges on white freshmen. The purpose, says Greer, is to make whites feel badly about their skin color. Whites should "sit down, shut up, and allow their moral superiors to berate them." An example is the "Whiteness" conference at the University of Michigan designed to help white students recognize their alleged privilege. This surrender by academia to identity politics is an insult to every American, including non-whites.

The *New York Post* exposed the Bank Street School, an elite private school in Manhattan where they are teaching white students as young as six that "they're born racist and should feel guilty about benefiting from white privilege," while their black peers are "taught to feel proud about their race and are rewarded with treats and other privileges." White parents have complained about how their children are indoctrinated into thinking that systemic racism still exists, that they are part of the problem, and that "any success they achieve is unearned." Parents are upset that the school "deliberately instills in white children a strong sense of guilt about their race." A six-year-old came home in tears, saying, "I'm a bad person." This is nothing short of disgusting.

The idea that white people are inherently flawed is absurd on its face. The value system that has made the US successful as a nation is an achievement of white people, especially white men. White men founded our republic. White men gave their lives to end slavery. White men are largely responsible for the day-to-day commerce that puts food on the table and clothing on our backs. America runs because of white people and their value system. Like it or not, white people drive the engine that makes this country work. In contrast, look at teenagers in the black subculture who hold themselves back by deliberately rejecting the values on which this country was founded. This self-destructive behavior—not white privilege—is ruining the lives of millions of black kids.

The payoff for the Left's diversity and multicultural agenda is stoking racial discord. Minority special interest groups are using the banners of "equality," "diversity," and "social justice" as a power grab. The intention is to impose their agenda on the white majority. It is a fight for equality only in the Orwellian sense. "All animals are equal," George Orwell wrote in *Animal Farm*, "but some animals are more equal than others." We are observing a grab for power by vocal minority groups who want to be more equal than others. Look out. If they succeed, they will institutionalize the inquisition.

LifeZette, January 9, 2018

NFL Kneeling—Racial Oppression at Ten Million Per Year

The president's criticism of NFL athletes' refusal to stand for the national anthem has come under attack on the grounds that (a) the players are calling out systemic racism, and (b) the president's comments are racist. Conservative pundits are defending the president's position with good arguments. Here are a few of them:

• *If professional athletes want to complain about racial inequality, they should say so instead of attacking the country and its flag.* If, as they say, they want to complain about how the police treat black suspects, protest THAT. Don't presume to take down the whole country as the object of protest.

• *Athletes do not have a constitutional right to express their political opinions on the field.* The First Amendment imposes restrictions on the federal government but not on individual employers' right to censor political expression by their employees while on the job. When you put on that uniform, you are representing the team, not your personal political viewpoint. If you have a gripe, get an interview on CNN. I'm sure they would love to have you.

• *The NFL's policies are not consistent.* It has imposed many restrictions on athletes' freedom of speech, not the least of which was denying the right to commemorate 9/11, but it selectively allows them to kneel during the national anthem. This is self-defeating, as it incurs the wrath of millions of fans. By insulting the president, Hollywood actors are doing the same thing and the movie industry is going to pay a heavy price as well.

These are good arguments, but the most compelling reasons for criticizing the protests are being overlooked. They are:

• *Systemic racism does not exist in the United States.* Individual instances of racism are occurring and always will occur—against both blacks and whites—but to suggest that racism is institutionalized is to deny the colossal changes that have occurred since the Civil Rights Movement of the 1960s. It was a big deal when Jackie Robinson broke the color line in baseball. Today, however, 70 percent of NFL players are black. We elected a black president TWICE. African-Americans are accorded special privileges—what I have referred to as "black privilege"—in every nook and cranny of our country. When an African-American athlete earning ten million a year attacks the system that is responsible for his incredible success, he is both ungrateful and hypocritical.

• *The Leftist canard that racist police and the justice system deliberately discriminate against African-Americans is a lie.* In 2017, it is ridiculous to suggest that white police are gunning for blacks. "The fault lies primarily with the black criminals," says political commentator Dennis Prager, "not with a racist society." The bulk of responsibility, agreed former New York Mayor Rudy Giuliani, is on African-Americans who "commit murder eight times more per capita than any other group in our society." Ignoring the obvious connection between black criminality and black incarceration, the Left continues to point a finger at the police. "Numerical disparities result from differences of offending," said black talk show host Larry Elder, "not because of racism."

• *The president's criticism of NFL athletes has nothing to do with race.* Introducing the race card is purely a contribution of the Left as part of its assault on American values and institutions. The mainstream media are attempting—unfairly—to portray Trump as racist, sexist, misogynistic, xenophobic, anti-Semitic, Islamophobic, etc. The chief strategy of the Democratic Party, says Harvard Law professor Alan Dershowitz, "is to use character assassination, otherwise referred to as 'the politics of personal destruction,' as the weapon of choice." The same lie was offered up by the Democrats to explain away the failure of Hillary Clinton's candidacy. It comes as no surprise that Mrs. Clinton has accused Trump of attacking black athletes. The weakness of the race card is that it is a feeble attempt to cover up the absence of any real arguments by the Left.

To the president's credit, he takes the offensive by calling out the media for what they are: fake. I like to contrast Trump with George W. Bush, whose silence allowed the media to portray him as intellectually deficient. Trump has a substantial portion of the country behind him because people are figuring out that they can't trust what they hear on CNN or read in the *New York Times*. They also understand that NFL athletes are showing contempt for the nation that enabled their success. The average American has difficulty swallowing the argument that millionaire athletes are being oppressed. Woe to the NFL as its ratings drop and fans find other pastimes to worship. Tennis anyone?

Clash Daily, September 26, 2017

White Privilege: The Big Lie About Race in America

The progressive liberal playbook includes a handful of concepts that are designed to enhance what I call the "tyranny of the minority"—the power of special interest groups achieved at the expense of the white majority. In addition to *social justice*, *diversity*, *multiculturalism*, and *toxic masculinity*, one of the most effective schemes invented by the Left is known as *white privilege*—a devious attempt to foment racial discord.

White privilege points to the unfairness of societal advantages that allegedly benefit all people identified as white. The Left wants white people to confess and atone for those advantages. It has been argued that white privilege, when abused, can lead to horrible crimes committed against society. Despite the rhetoric, the white privilege argument is nothing more than a racist attack on Caucasians. "The fact that white people are better off is not a privilege," says David Horowitz, author of *Black Skin Privilege and the American Dream*. "It's earned," he insists. The value system that has made the U.S. successful as a nation is an achievement of white people, especially white men. White men founded our republic. White men gave their lives to end slavery. The efforts of white men are largely responsible for the day-to-day commerce that puts food on the table and clothing on our backs. Like it or not, white people drive the engine that makes this country work.

If we wanted to be truthful about the causes of social disruption in the U.S., we would have to point a finger not at white America but rather at the African-American community. In spite of a continuing history of violence, blacks are not being held accountable for their behavior. It is not politically correct to criticize African-Americans, and if you attempt to do so, you are automatically labeled a racist. There is no question that blacks lag behind other groups in economic success, safe neighborhoods, education, and family cohesiveness. The question is, who or what is responsible?

The Left insists that the blame belongs squarely on the shoulders of white people. Not so, says David Horowitz. It is not white privilege that's preventing blacks from doing better, Horowitz argues. It's African-American behavior, such as the propensity to commit violent crimes, the inability to build more intact families, and the unwillingness to accept personal responsibility. Black women do not take responsibility for having children out of wedlock and black fathers do not take responsibility for raising their children. Many teenagers in the black subculture hold themselves back by deliberately rejecting mainstream values. This self-destructive behavior—not white privilege—is ruining the lives of millions of black kids.

Wall Street Journal editorial board member Jason Riley has accused civil rights leaders of being more interested in "blaming the problems of blacks on white racism" than getting to the real causes. Political commentator Bill O'Reilly agrees that acceptance of the white privilege argument is encouraging blacks not to take personal responsibility. When you realize that this negative value is already a cancer in black America, blaming white people only compounds an existing problem. Even white Americans are falling for the white privilege scam, says O'Reilly. They are "making excuses for bad behavior," he says, and "enabling the chaos" in places like Chicago.

Because they depend on the black vote, the Democrats won't do anything—such as telling the truth—that might offend the African-American community. Instead, the myth of white privilege is being used to brainwash a generation of Americans.

Schools across the country are carrying out a racial inquisition where white students are given tests that force them to admit to their so-called white privilege. White students as young as six are taught that they are born racist and should feel guilty that any success they achieve is unearned. Many colleges are forcing white freshmen to take indoctrination courses designed to make them feel badly about their skin color, reports Scott Greer in *No Campus for White Men*. Greer describes these classes as demonstrating "an outright hatred for white people, especially white men."

Instead of unfairly shaming white students, what we really need are indoctrination courses to help minority students take personal responsibility. In blaming white people for all the ills of society, the values of our educational system are upside-down. The very notion of white privilege ought to be an insult to the intelligence of every American. It is a fantasy concocted so white Americans can be demonized and black Americans can avoid dealing truthfully with their issues. For the sake of our children, we must come to our senses before we wind up with a generation of racially confused neurotics.

Clash Daily, January 15, 2018

Black Privilege: What the Media Won't Tell You

In previous books and articles, I have attempted to debunk "white privilege"—a bigoted concept pointing to the unfairness of societal privileges that allegedly benefit all people identified as white.

Whatever those privileges may have been in the past, they are no longer prevalent in today's America. "More whites have begun talking about themselves as a racially oppressed majority," reports CNN. "In a widely publicized 2011 survey, white Americans said they suffer from racial discrimination more than blacks."

White privilege attempts to relieve minorities, especially African-Americans, of responsibility for the problems in their respective communities by placing the blame on a so-called tradition of white racism. The justification given for white privilege is that America is a racist nation bent on oppressing its minorities. White privilege is in itself a racist doctrine.

Heather Mac Donald, author of *The War on Cops*, contends that the bottom line question is: *Should African-Americans be held responsible for their own behavior—including criminal behavior, or are they victims of a racist society?* Mac Donald and I are in agreement that blacks cannot shirk responsibility for their own behavior. The notion that African-Americans are victims of a racist society may have been true prior to the 1960s, but this is a half-century after the Civil Rights Movement. "White institutional racism has disappeared from our society," says Scott Greer in *No Campus for White Men*. "Black Americans now have every opportunity that white Americans have long enjoyed."

Actually, in today's America, the tables have turned. What we are witnessing now is *black privilege*. African-Americans are accorded special treatment across the board. "Victim status is treasured in America," says Ben Shapiro, "and black skin guarantees automatic victim status thanks to America's history." Being black today, Shapiro concludes, grants privileges ranging from landing coveted college scholarships to becoming activists who can build careers on racial grievances. Here are some examples of black privilege:

• Affirmative action quotas are the norm in education and employment, "more firmly entrenched in our society than ever before," says Scott Greer.

• Political correctness supports anything related to African-Americans and condemns anything related to Caucasian-Americans.

• College and university courses are specially designed for black students.

• Black students benefit from the lower standards applied by college professors who practice "affirmative grading."

• Corporate diversity programs—CNN reports that corporations offer special programs and internships to black workers but not to whites.

• Diversity training portrays blacks in a positive light and whites negatively.

• Many courts are reluctant to prosecute blacks for various criminal acts in fear of being called racist.

• Blacks can belong to clubs and organizations that cater specifically to their race, reports CNN, "but there's no National Association for the Advancement of White People because such a group would be deemed racist."

• Media bias caters to positive depictions of blacks and avoids negative ones.

- "Black pride" is considered a form of empowerment; "white pride" is considered a form of racism.

- Blacks can get away with racial slurs, but whites can't use the N word.

- Hollywood casting has completely turned around as a consequence of aggressive lobbying by black special interests.

- Black privilege even extends to the White House, observes author David Horowitz, alleging that Obama "wouldn't be elected dogcatcher if he wasn't black."

The white establishment is bending over backwards to accommodate African-Americans who demonstrate even marginal capabilities. You won't see that happen in the NBA, which is based on performance, but the rest of our society has ceased to be a meritocracy. Given the enormous strides we have made on the issue of race, black privilege is no longer justified. On its face, it is just as racist as white privilege.

The Left is delighted with black privilege because it helps to destroy the important American value known as taking personal responsibility. Progressive liberals would rather see low-income blacks dependent on big government, trapped in the tentacles of the welfare state. By expecting little from African-Americans, the government has promoted what I call a *victim mentality*: the unwillingness to take responsibility for one's own behavior and instead blaming others (white people, for example) for life's problems.

Black privilege, in the long run, perpetuates the victim mentality. It is just not going to be good for anyone, regardless of skin color.

Daily Surge, April 18, 2017

Open Season on White People—The New Politics of Racism

The big scandal last week was that *New York Times* editorial board member Sarah Jeong tweeted "cancel white people," "white men are bullshit," and "dumbass f---ing white people," and bragged that she enjoys "being cruel to old white men." Political commentator Bill O'Reilly says Jeong's tweets are consistent with the *Times*' editorial philosophy that "white men have destroyed the country." It comes as no surprise to anyone who has been watching current social trends. Today's Caucasians, especially males, are being demonized and marginalized by the Left and its media enablers.

The Left, says author Ben Shapiro, wants to portray America as "an incurable mass of bigoted whites." One of the racist arguments advocated by the Left is "white privilege," the notion that society bestows unfair advantages to all people identified as white. For this reason, Democrats have justified open borders as a means of diminishing the percentage of the U.S. population that is white. A surprising number of white apologists support this nonsense.

Author David Horowitz is appalled by blatant anti-white racism. "The fact that white people are better off is not a privilege," he says. "It's earned." White men founded our republic, white men ended slavery, and white men are largely responsible for the day-to-day commerce that puts food on the table and clothing on our backs. America runs because of white people and their value system. Like it or not, white people drive the engine that makes this country work.

In contrast, teenagers in the black subculture abhor the very idea of adopting white values. The worst insult for these kids is to be called "whitey" or "Uncle Tom." This self-destructive behavior—not white privilege—is ruining the lives of millions of African-American kids. Their value system is marked by anger, violence, and refusal to accept personal responsibility. It is reinforced by political correctness, which bashes white people and white values at every opportunity.

More and more people have figured out that the old excuses for black crime and violence—jobs, poverty, schooling, etc.—are no longer valid. "Now they have a new excuse," says Colin Flaherty in *Don't Make the Black Kids Angry*. "The ultimate excuse: White racism is everywhere. White racism is permanent. White racism explains everything." Blaming the problems of the black community on white racism is false, as African-American author Shelby Steele has pointed out. "The oppression of black Americans is over with," Steele recently explained on Fox News' *Life, Liberty and Levin*. "White institutional racism has disappeared from our society," agrees author Scott Greer in *No Campus for White Men*.

Anti-white sentiment is especially virulent in colleges and universities. Identity politics on campus, says Scott Greer, is "increasingly bordering on outright hatred for white people, especially white men." Bashing white people is acceptable to the Left, adds Ben Shapiro, because they believe that racism can only come from dominant groups. Only whites can be bigots. Non-white people cannot be bigots. So if Sarah Jeong attacks white people, the Left claims it is not actually racism.

Anti-white attacks are an offshoot of the Left's preoccupation with its perverted version of "diversity," where Americans are divided between oppressors—heterosexual, white, Christian males—and victimized groups of minorities and women. Minority groups are said to need protection because they are oppressed by the white majority. This is the victimhood culture of today's college campus, says Scott Greer, where whites are morally inferior and blacks are superior because of their presumed history of oppression. "It is the old Marxist wine in new bottles," says David Horowitz in *Big Agenda*, "and the results are bound to be similar."

Instead of making everyone feel they are part of a unified American social structure, diversity plays into the leftist strategy of "divide and conquer." With its emphasis on diversity, says Mark Levin in *Ameritopia*, the Left achieves the "balkanization" of society. Its version of diversity means the opposite of the traditional motto of the United States, "e pluribus unum." Out of many, one. Wherever you came from, whatever you were, you are American now. The Left wants it to read, "Out of one, many." For the Left, the whole purpose of diversity is division. For the rest of us, "It has not been our diversity," said African-American author Thomas Sowell, "but our ability to overcome the problems inherent in diversity, and to act together as Americans, that has been our strength."

White America has been mostly passive about the blitz of anti-white rhetoric—perhaps because of white guilt, perhaps because of fear of violent reprisals, perhaps because so many people are uninformed. At the same time, "More whites have begun talking about themselves as a racially oppressed majority," reports CNN. "In a widely publicized 2011 survey, white Americans said they suffer from racial discrimination more than blacks." It is time to declare that white people are victimized by racism and ought to be designated as a special class. Someone should explain to "people of color" that white is a color too.

Clash Daily, August 8, 2018

Rush to Judgment with Phony Charges of Racism

An experience I had in 2008 was prophetic. When some people who were supposed to be my friends discovered that I was not voting for Obama, they joined voices to call me a racist. I didn't know it then, but their behavior was the wave of the future. We have two new examples of what has become commonplace—irresponsible calling out of racism by the mainstream media and the political Left. First is the case of David Webb being accused of white privilege. The second concerns a group of admirable young white men falsely accused of racism against Native Americans.

The David Webb case would be funny if it were not revealing of the witch hunts being conducted by our stalwart progressive journalists in the media. On a radio talk show, CNN "legal analyst" Areva Martin, who is black, disagreed with the conservative ideas expressed by show host David Webb. As Webb later pointed out, instead of dealing with the substance of his opinions, Martin immediately defaulted to the white privilege argument. When she accused Webb of having white privilege, he responded in a way Martin never expected.

Webb: *"How do I have the privilege of white privilege?"*

Martin: *"David, by virtue of being a white male you have white privilege."*

Webb: *"I hate to break it to you, but you should've been better prepped. I'm black."*

Talk about having egg on your face! If I were Ms. Martin, I would find a deserted island and hide out under a rock. Oddly, she doesn't appear to be fazed by the incident at all. To Martin's way of looking at it, calling someone a racist is her prerogative.

The Left supports her. In the 1950s, the worst thing you could say about someone was, "You're a communist!" Today it is, "You're a racist!" Ironically, white privilege is a racist attack on white people.

Wall Street Journal editorial board member Jason Riley, who is also black, understands the purpose of the white privilege argument. Riley has accused civil rights leaders of being more interested in "blaming the problems of blacks on white racism" than getting to the real causes. Political commentator Bill O'Reilly agrees that acceptance of the white privilege argument is encouraging blacks not to take personal responsibility. When you realize that unwillingness to accept personal responsibility is already a cancer in black America, blaming white people only compounds an existing problem. Even white Americans are falling for the white privilege scam, says O'Reilly. They are "making excuses for bad behavior," he says, and "enabling the chaos" in places like Chicago.

Because they depend on the black vote, the Democrats won't do anything—such as telling the truth—that might offend the African-American community. Instead, the myth of white privilege is being used to brainwash a generation of Americans. Schools across the country are carrying out a racial inquisition where white students are subjected to tests that force them to admit to their so-called white privilege. White students as young as six are taught that they are born racist and should feel guilty that any success they achieve is unearned. Many colleges are forcing white freshmen to take indoctrination courses designed to make them feel badly about their skin color, reports Scott Greer in *No Campus for White Men*. Greer describes these classes as demonstrating "an outright hatred for white people, especially white men."

Ms. Martin's rush to judgment about David Webb's skin color is standard issue for left-leaning journalists. But wait. Webb's experience pales in comparison to the ordeal imposed by the media on Nick Sandmann and other teenage boys from a Catholic high school in Kentucky. As reported by the media, the boys assaulted Nathan Phillips, a 64-year-old "Native American" and alleged Vietnam veteran. The media accused them of racism. So did a battalion of politicians, celebrities, and your Aunt Minnie. Everybody rushed to get on the bandwagon. Sandmann not only assaulted Phillips, it was reported, he continued to "smirk" at the poor elderly gentleman. "It was ugly, what these kids were involved in," Phillips said. "It was racism. It was hatred. It was scary." Everyone agreed that such behavior by privileged white youths must be condemned. Sandmann and his parents have received death threats. The Catholic Diocese of Covington, Kentucky, issued an apology and promised to take "appropriate action, up to and including expulsion." The boys were a disgraceful example of white racism at work, end of discussion.

Fortunately for Sandmann and his buddies, it was not the end of the discussion. Mr. Sandmann composed an articulate defense in which he describes himself as the victim and Phillips as the aggressor. And guess what? Several videos have surfaced that completely confirm Sandmann's statement. The episode was apparently set in motion because the boys were wearing Make America Great Again hats. Their sartorial choice offended many who were present and evidently sparked insults and the aggressive behavior of Mr. Phillips, who has lied about the whole affair. Thank goodness for the videos. Without the videos, a great lie would have been accepted and the lives of the boys would have been ruined.

Here is what really happened: As the boys were minding their own business during a visit to Washington, DC, they were confronted—perhaps assaulted is the correct word—by Phillips, who got right up in Sandmann's face while beating a drum and chanting something unintelligible. Phillips' Native American companions said the boys "stole our land" and told the boys to "go back to Europe." A group of nearby black men called the boys "racists," "bigots," "white crackers," and "incest kids." Sandmann, unaware of what was happening, stood his ground but kept his mouth shut. His forbearance should have elicited praise. Instead, he and the other boys were accused of racism. Phillips, his co-protestors, and the group of black men were guilty of Trump Derangement Syndrome. It had nothing to do with racism. It was all about the red hats.

Sandmann exercised more restraint and maturity than I would have in similar circumstances. "I believed that by remaining motionless and calm, I was helping to diffuse the situation," Sandmann said. "I realized everyone had cameras and that perhaps a group of adults was trying to provoke a group of teenagers into a larger conflict." Sounds like a great kid, someone to be proud of. He is owed an apology from all who rushed to judgment, including the media, Mr. Phillips, and Sandmann's own diocese. But don't hold your breath. Even with all the evidence to the contrary, many are still calling Sandmann a racist. That's how it is these days. Get used to it.

Clash Daily, January 22, 2019

Chapter 9: Sexual Politics

Should Allegations of Sexual Abuse Be Taken Seriously?

In the 1948 movie, *The Adventures of Don Juan*, Errol Flynn plays the infamous Spanish lover. When he is accused of making advances to a married woman, Don Juan/Flynn is defended by a courtier who testifies that the woman asked for it. "A man can only take so much," says the eyewitness, suggesting that the don should not be faulted for succumbing to the aggressive moves of a seductive female. This movie sequence can serve as a metaphor for the current rash of sexual misconduct allegations.

We have a similar accusation that President Trump pushed a woman "up against the wall" at Mar-a-Lago and "had his hands all over" her. I can say from personal experience that most men will not behave like this unless they have received positive reinforcement from a woman. In this case, we don't know what provoked the alleged "pushing up against the wall" but you can take it from me that if Trump is guilty as charged, which I doubt, it is likely that the "victim" encouraged the behavior. Trump is insightful and socially adept, hardly the kind of man who would initiate unwanted sexual advances. So even if the allegation is true, a determination of wrongdoing cannot be made without taking into consideration the surrounding circumstances. Geraldo Rivera nailed it when he tweeted that the "current epidemic of sex harassment allegations may be criminalizing courtship and conflating it with predation."

And so we come to the main issue, the assertion by a group of women in the Congress that all allegations of sexual misconduct must be "taken seriously." What they really are suggesting is that when a woman accuses a man of sexual abuse, he should be deemed guilty without proof or evidence of wrongdoing. The word of the accuser ought to be enough to convict even when the only evidence is, "I told my girlfriend 40 years ago." This suggestion shows contempt for the guiding principle of our legal system that you are innocent until proven guilty. Many reputations and careers of successful men are being destroyed strictly on the basis of unsubstantiated allegations. This is a form of sexual McCarthyism and should be discouraged instead of defended by the court of public opinion.

It all boils down to what behaviors are to be labeled as sexual misconduct. For example, a former Congressional aide complained that when she was 22, a congressman told her she looked great, then asked her to twirl around. And that's all. He did not grope her, kiss her, fondle her, try to screw her, or ask her to watch him masturbate. It is the story of an older man paying a compliment to a young girl, and nothing more. Yet the media have agreed that this constitutes sexual misconduct. The infamous video of Trump talking about women is another case in point. He never says in the video that he forced himself on a woman. He says that when you are a celebrity, "they let you do" whatever you want. He is referring to consensual sex. His attackers claim he admits to being a sexual predator, an assertion that is not supported by the video.

In the case of dismissed Fox News star Bill O'Reilly, none of the allegations against him has been proven. One accuser was upset because O'Reilly referred to her as "hot chocolate." Another accuser was angry because he advised her to show more cleavage. O'Reilly may be guilty of coarse manners, but that does not make him a predator. A former beauty contestant experienced mental anguish because Trump allegedly "looked her up and down." If she was so sensitive about being recognized for her physical attributes, what the hell was she doing in a beauty pageant? And what about the woman who said Matt Lauer asked her to unbutton her blouse? She did as he requested. If he didn't force her, why did she do it? Why did she then have sex with him? Could it be that she used Lauer in order to advance her career? Geraldo Rivera and Pamela Anderson have been criticized for arguing that women need to take responsibility for their own behavior.

An instructive example is the case of movie actress Salma Hayek, who wrote an indignant letter to the *New York Times* accusing Harvey Weinstein of terrible behavior, of treating her unfairly, of forcing her to do a sex scene in a movie, and of being a "monster." Although I am not defending Weinstein, he did not rape Ms. Hayek. He was, quite simply, behaving badly. In Hayek's case, a strong argument can be made that she deliberately accepted the Weinstein treatment in order to get what she wanted. In fact, if you Google "Salma Hayek" you will find dozens of photos of the actress in compromising positions that suggest her morals are not very different from Weinstein's. Is Harvey responsible for the lurid photos of Hayek? I don't think so. This is not some little angel we are dealing with. When you are willing to do anything to advance your career, you should think twice about accusing someone else of sexual misconduct.

It must be acknowledged that all people experience unfair behavior. It is not pleasant, but it is not illegal. It is part of life. You deal with it as best you can and then you move on. Unfortunately, the "me too" lynchings ignore this fact of life. Instead, accusations of sexual abuse are being used as political weapons. It has just been made public that women's rights attorney Lisa Bloom "tried to line up big paydays" for women who were willing to accuse Donald Trump of sexual misconduct during the final months of the presidential election. According to *The Hill*, Bloom worked with campaign donors and media outlets to arrange compensation for the "victims" and a commission for herself when their stories sold to the media. In one case, an accuser was offered $750,000 to go public. These reports suggest that women are capable of fabricating their stories for personal gain or revenge. An eye-opening example is the case of Gemma Beale, whose false rape accusations led to the two-year incarceration of an innocent man in the UK.

Should all allegations of sexual misconduct be taken seriously? Yes, but they should also be thoroughly investigated before we jump to conclusions and ruin the careers of admirable men...and women.

Daily Surge, December 18, 2017

The Women's March: Decent People Seduced by the Left

Barack Obama used his devious "Hope and Change" mantra—masking a socialist, anti-American agenda—to seduce millions of "liberal" voters. After eight years, the electorate finally awakened from the nightmare that was Obama. His agenda—the Left's agenda—was voted down in the 2016 presidential election. No matter. The Left wants to perpetuate its values by whatever means are necessary. For the Left, the end justifies the means. They don't care what we—the people who voted for Trump—think. The Left is against individual rights and the rule of law. The Left is totalitarian. They want to revert back to the socialist model and to hell with what the voters have to say about it.

Enter the "Women's March." Women from across the nation have descended on Washington to protest their victimhood. The Left has frightened these decent women, telling them that their reproductive rights are being taken away by the Republicans. Once they accept this argument, the marchers fall into line and buy into the entire leftist agenda. The Women's March is a tribute to the gullibility of large segments of our population. Ostensibly the women are marching for women's rights, but in reality it is all about fringe liberal movements that aim to ride roughshod over the majority. Look at the predominance of the disaffected among the list of speakers: Angela Davis, Van Jones, Gloria Steinem, Michael Moore. Listen to the angry, vicious hate speech ... all in the name of "love."

What do these Leftists want? Moore revealed the truth when he said that "what we need" in government are women (i.e., liberal women), blacks, Hispanics, gays, transgenders, etc. Falsely posing as a movement of inclusion, *this is a movement of exclusion.* Men, heterosexuals, and conservative women are distinctly not wanted. I can hear Elizabeth Warren screaming, "We've had it with guys like you!" The Left does not want alpha males like Donald Trump. They want feminized men like Michael Moore. And what kind of women do they want? Warren, Hillary Clinton, Nancy Pelosi, Maxine Waters, Kamala Harris.

President Trump is portrayed as misogynistic, racist, anti-Semitic. Rachel Maddow on MSNBC compared Trump to Adolf Hitler. The majority of voters don't buy all this nonsense, but the *New York Times* does. The Women's March should take out a full-page ad in the *Times* that says, "The best man for the job is a woman." Let's face it, they are angry that a woman was not elected president.

The anti-Trump hysteria has been cooked up by the Left, supported by the left-leaning mainstream media, and swallowed whole by decent women who seem to be living in denial of reality. Frankly, I am sympathetic to the pro-choice position, but today's reality is that abortion is no longer the main issue facing the country. Immigration and Islamic terrorism are the big issues. The Women's March accuses Trump of discrimination against Mexicans and Muslims because he wants to protect our borders. He is accused of anti-black racism because he believes in the rule of law. The organizers of the march would like to see millions of illegal aliens pouring across the Rio Grande accompanied by riots and looting in the black communities.

And so now we come to the real hypocrisy of the Women's March. By taking the position that Trump is a racist, their intention is to further divide a country that is already suffering from the divisive policies of the Obama administration. By taking a position against "Islamophobia," they are condoning the planet's number one abuser of women: Islam. If these women want to protest policies and behaviors that disregard women's rights, why don't they go after the treatment of women under the banner of the Islamic religion? As Kay Hymowitz wrote in *City Journal*: "Where are the demonstrations, the articles, the petitions, the resolutions, the vindications of the rights of Islamic women by American feminists?"

There is an obvious reason for this hypocrisy. If they would speak out against the treatment of women under Islam, feminists would be obliged to acknowledge the progress that has been made for women's rights in the West. That would detract from their coveted victim status. By keeping quiet, feminists are colluding with Muslims who want to bring Sharia to our shores. Here lies the sad irony about the Women's March. Instead of improving the condition of women, the Leftist agenda ultimately would destroy all the gains made by women in the past half century.

Daily Surge, January 23, 2017

Toxic Femininity—A Male Perspective

Branding men with undesirable character traits has turned into a popular sport. Men are considered by some—a vocal few, at least—to be competitive, aggressive, and violent, while women are thought of as passive and more inclined to collaboration. As an unrepentant male, I take umbrage at the increasing references to "toxic masculinity." There are two reasons. First, I believe this is pure sexism driven by a small but angry cadre of power-hungry radical feminists. I can see no earthly reason that would require me to defend the values and behavior of my sex. Second, my basic sense of fairness resents the fact that men are often demonized while women get a free pass. If we are going to have a conversation about toxic masculinity, equal time should be devoted to "toxic femininity."

What is toxic femininity? Does our typical female bear the burden of undesirable character traits? "Sentimental insistence on female innocence," suggests the *New York Times*, "does no service to women, who should be treated as human beings with a capacity for aggression and held equally accountable for their actions." Here are ten characteristics of toxic femininity:

1. *Male-directed anger and paranoia*: Many contemporary women actively dislike the male of the species. Ask the average man. He will tell you that a lot of women are just plain angry at men. They love to hold men accountable for all women's problems. If a hurtful motivation can be attributed to men, women will go for it. Some are angry because they have convinced themselves that men perceive women strictly as sex objects. For many, feminism is synonymous with demonization of men.

160

2. *Transference neurosis*: This is an unconscious defense mechanism where a woman's feelings and attitudes originally associated with male authority figures earlier in her life are attributed or redirected to others in the present. A good example is the unreasonable hatred many women have for President Trump. The transference takes place when Trump—the ultimate male authority figure—is substituted for the bad father, husband, boyfriend, etc. "Angry woman syndrome" is another label given to this condition, where a woman's negative past experiences create obstacles to current relationships.

3. *Gender manipulation*: Women have become adept at passive-aggressive "bitchy" behavior and hidden agendas used to manipulate men. "Men's brains are designed to spend their time figuring out how to get objects in the environment to do their bidding," says *angryharry.com*. "Women's brains are designed to spend their time figuring out how to get men to do their bidding." According to *Fox News*, female manipulation can manifest itself as "dressing sexy," withholding sex and affection, and flirting with other men. Without blinking an eye, a woman may compromise her integrity for money and security, the ultimate form of gender manipulation.

4. *Emotional detachment*: It seems that women are less dependent on relationships than men. Many women are "unwilling or incapable to commit completely to a relationship," says *match.com*. "The reasons for this can be quite complex, ranging from emotional trauma to a simple matter of priorities, where a woman is more focused on her career than a relationship." According to *The Telegraph*, the number of female sociopaths is rising: "cruel, calculating and calm under pressure."

5. *Female victimization*: Many women play the victim as a method of controlling men. The "damsel in distress" persona has

created a sense of entitlement. "Poor me." "I deserve to be taken care of." "I gave you the best years of my life." "Women are not paid the same as men." "There is a war on women."

6. *The "superwoman" delusion*: Thanks to the feminist movement, women have been saddled with the idea that "you can do it all." You can have success at both family and career, with no exceptions. This is a huge burden. Heaven help the woman who is satisfied to be a housewife.

7. *Female self-hatred*: Most women are depressed by what they see in the mirror. They hate themselves for not living up to impossible standards of physical beauty. This "self-loathing" in women can lead to depression, suicidal feelings, and related eating disorders such as obesity, bulimia, and anorexia.

8. *Avoidance of accountability*: It has become socially acceptable for women to deny responsibility for their actions. In the movie *As Good As It Gets*, Jack Nicholson explains his success at writing fictional women characters. "I think of a man," he says, "and then I take away reason and accountability."

9. *Vicious competition with other women*: "Women compete, compare, undermine and undercut one another," says the *New York Times*. "Feeling on guard around other ladies is normal for a lot of women." Evolution has made women wary of their sisters as they compete for male attention or in the workplace. "A host of studies in recent years has shown convincingly that the traditional view of women as passive and uncompetitive is wrong," says *Psychology Today*. "Women, it turns out, are engaged in a competition of their own, aggressively jockeying for position in a battle to secure a suitable mate."

10. *Female martyr syndrome*: We are witnessing many examples of individual women pretending to speak for all women when

they are only expressing their own opinion. Recent examples in the news are Gloria Steinem, Madeleine Albright, Ashley Judd, and Madonna. The irony is that these women typically lead privileged lifestyles and so have difficulty relating to "average" women.

Colleges and universities are giving men a forum to examine their allegedly toxic behavior patterns. Fairness demands that we consider the following:

• Equivalent college courses giving women the opportunity to confront their toxic femininity.

• Hollywood films that describe how both sexes are suffering because of women's gender-related shortcomings.

• More alternative life choices for women in order to relieve the intolerable pressure arising from the superwoman delusion.

• A provision in healthcare insurance for psychotherapy to help women overcome their transference neurosis.

If we can encourage women to spend more time looking inward, we may enjoy a reprieve from the anger that has characterized the women's movement from its inception.

Daily Caller, February 13, 2017

Social Engineering Will Kill the Marines

My alma mater, the US Marine Corps, was embroiled this week in a noisy scandal. A group of Marines has been accused of posting nude photos of female service members on the Internet. The scandal has resulted in a hue-and-cry from all directions. It must be a hot item because even media-freak Gloria Allred has become involved. Gen. Robert Neller, Commandant of the Marine Corps, reacted by saying that the allegations "undermine everything that we stand for as a Marine Corps, and as Marines: discipline, honor, professionalism, and respect and trust amongst each other." In a strict sense, Gen. Neller is correct. We should not excuse the actions of the Marines who are responsible for this fiasco. But in a broader context, Marines do not deserve blame for what is really one of the unfortunate consequences of applying political correctness to our military.

President Obama included among his many dubious "social engineering" objectives the enforcement by the federal government of the arbitrary imperatives of political correctness. One of his progressive notions was that women in the military must enjoy complete equality with men. Instead of strengthening a weakened military—his primary duty as commander-in-chief—Obama evidently believed that it was more important to open all combat jobs to women. Assigning women to front line units raises two issues: (1) Can women hold up their end in combat units? (2) What effect will this have on morale?

In response to the first question, Marine Corps Gen. Joseph Dunford, chairman of the Joint Chiefs of Staff, stood up in opposition to Obama's policy. Dunford has voiced concerns about potential impacts on combat readiness. The only service to seek an exemption to gender integration, the Marines have found that men outperform women in a variety of ground-combat tasks, and that all-male units perform better than mixed-gender units. Although a small percentage of women can measure up to Marine Corps combat standards, most cannot. So far, no Women Marines have passed the difficult Infantry Officer Course, even though dozens have tried. Let's hope this does not lead to lowering the current standards.

The bigger picture, as raised by the second question, concerns the realities of military recruitment. No one in his—or her—right mind is going to voluntarily place himself in harm's way by signing up for combat duty. Asking citizens to put their lives in jeopardy is, and has always been, a major problem for governments. The solution for armies over the millennia has been using the appeal of "male macho" to outweigh common sense and the desire for self-preservation. Throughout history, armed forces have attracted male volunteers based on a macho war ethic. Nowhere is this more evident today than in our country's elite fighting force, the Marine Corps. Young men want to be Marines because they respond to the slogan, "The few. The proud. The Marines." I know. I did.

Now for the first time in our history, the government is saying that you don't have to be a tough macho man to occupy a foxhole. Women can do it. No big deal. "If women can join the few and the proud," many men are thinking, "being a Marine is no longer a proclamation of my manhood. Why should I risk my life to prove that I am a tough guy?" Removing the payoff for being macho is upsetting the psychological underpinning of the entire defense apparatus. The effect on the male subconscious of putting women in front line units cannot be underestimated. We can expect to see three serious consequences: (1) a drastic reduction in male voluntary enlistments, (2) the premature retirement or outright firing of senior officers who refuse to play ball with the PC crowd, and (3) the acting out of anti-social behaviors by elite troops. Political correctness, if allowed to spread, will eventually erode our military effectiveness. Evidently Obama never considered this possibility when he insisted on a PC-compliant Defense Department. Or did he?

The current Marine Corps scandal is but one example of unforeseen collateral damage that will result from the new gender policy. In order to protect their male egos, Marines and other elite troops are going to exhibit a variety of behaviors that will not be regarded as socially acceptable. In the current scandal, Marines are subconsciously protecting their macho-ness by posting the nude photos. As in Post Traumatic Stress Disorder (PTSD), the fault does not lie with the individual Marine. The fault belongs to Obama's efforts to eviscerate the military. Happily, the new administration may reverse Obama's policy. *Military Times* reports that President Trump has been a vocal skeptic of political correctness in the Defense Department.

One final irony. According to *CBS News*, "Pentagon officials say the scandal can do real harm to the military by discouraging young women from joining the armed forces and convincing those already in uniform to get out." As usual, the media has it all wrong. The "real harm to the military" is the way in which political correctness and social engineering may discourage young men from signing up to fight for their country.

Daily Caller, March 13, 2017

Why Women Hate Trump

President Donald J. Trump is not only the answer to the prayers of conservatives, he is also the solution to the psychological problems of millions of American women. Oh, you thought the solution was electing the first female president? Not at all. Let me explain.

Many women are using the current political climate as an opportunity to reveal that they were victims of abuse by male authority figures. "Women who I have seen for years are only now bringing up physical and sexual trauma from their past," says Atlanta psychotherapist Melissa Olson. "I think this election is re-traumatizing them. Verbal and emotional abuse, sexual abuse, rape, discrimination … There have been many reminders of experiences that so many of us have had." These women are transferring the painful feelings associated with their traumatic experiences to the president, who serves as a convenient substitute for the original male authority figure in their lives.

This unconscious defense mechanism is known in psychiatry as *transference*, or *transference neurosis*, where feelings and attitudes originally associated with important people and events in one's early life are attributed or redirected to others in the present. "Others" in this case refers to the ultimate authority figure and alpha male, President Trump.

Women are coming out of the woodwork to express their outrage against Trump. They say he is a misogynist and sexual predator who has abused women by grabbing their vaginas. His objective, they insist, is to take away women's rights. They are angry that a sexual predator has risen to the post of commander-in-chief. While I empathize with the pain of these trauma victims,

I cannot condone their lack of judgment in substituting Trump for their abusive father or husband or uncle or whomever.

The charge that Trump is a sexual predator is totally unfounded. It is based on false allegations made by Hillary Clinton's presidential campaign and perpetuated by the mainstream media. The evidence is strictly circumstantial: an 11-year-old video in which Trump uses some off-color language under the mistaken assumption that the microphones are turned off; referring to Clinton as a "nasty woman"; calling a former Miss Universe "Miss Piggy"; threatening to sue women who have claimed that Trump assaulted them. On the infamous video, Trump says, "When you're a star, they let you do it. You can do anything." Trump is describing *consensual sex*. He never says he grabbed a woman's crotch without her consent. Enjoying consensual sex does not disqualify anyone from serving as president.

Unfortunately, as in so many examples of political correctness, the facts do not assuage the anger. Consider the out-of-control rage expressed by actress Ashley Judd in her tantrum at the Women's March in Washington: screaming that Trump is Hitler in disguise, that Trump is having incest with his daughter, that he is guilty of racism, homophobia, fraud, white supremacy, and on and on. How convenient it is to have someone like Trump upon whom to focus all of your accumulated angst. But convenience does not add up to "right" or "justified" or "appropriate."

Judd and other participants in the Women's March want to act out their anger in violent and destructive ways. I call this *emotional vandalism*. They don't care about facts because they have been transformed from adults into adult children who are interested only in their feelings, with contempt for the feelings of others. "Dysfunctional anger does not help us to do the right thing," says New York psychologist Robert Fraum. "Dysfunctional anger can be destructive, out of proportion, and inappropriate to the circumstances."

An example of emotional vandalism is offered by the *Huffington Post*:

> "Right now you've got a lot of angry women to contend with. And let me remind you, Mr. Trump ... hell hath no fury like a pissed off woman who's tired of this sexist bullshit. We are calling you out, Mr. Trump. We will not go quietly into any good night. We are loud. We are in your face. And we don't put up with the kind of bullshit you're selling. We see your sexism and your bigotry and your racism. We see right through you."

In response, a female Trump supporter said, "I think it's great, do your thing, but I just don't know what they're doing it for. They're talking about rights, women's rights, but what rights are being taken away from any women?" The point is that no rights are being taken away from any woman by the president. It may be healthy for women to enjoy a catharsis from their psychic pain, but it is not healthy when they transfer that pain to the highest office in the land. Taking into consideration that the entire argument against Trump is based on falsehood, it also constitutes serious male bashing.

What is the practical alternative? A few years of serious psychotherapy would help. In a supportive therapeutic environment, someone like Ashley Judd can explore reasons why her destructive transference occurs and help prevent its recurrence without resorting to extreme behavior.

Daily Surge, February 6, 2017

Sex is Dirty Again: Return of the Good Old Victorian Era

The Victorian Era in England and America was known for intolerant attitudes toward sexual matters. The Victorian standard of personal morality was simple: sex is taboo. People did not discuss sex and pretended they did not have sex. It was just dirty. Although Queen Victoria died in 1901, the prudish era named after her lasted well into the 1960s. (Why do you suppose that Ken and Barbie are missing their genitals?) From the 1960s until recently, we have experienced a period of sexual freedom and experimentation.

Well guess what. The good old Victorian Era is making a comeback. Courtesy of "MeToo," anything remotely sexual is taboo once again. All attempts by men to manifest their natural sex drive can be interpreted as sexual misconduct and men are guilty until proven innocent. In fact, proof of innocence is irrelevant. Witch hunts against innocent men are common. The careers of public figures are destroyed by malicious rumors. Republican Senator Roger Wicker was "roundly criticized" when all he did was call some teenage pages "beautiful girls." Aziz Ansari, a Muslim comedian (if there is such a thing), had a date with a woman who was excited to go out with him because he was a celebrity. When he attempted to have sex with her, she jumped at the opportunity but after the fact decided that she really wasn't that sort of girl. This hypocritical woman's charge of sexual misconduct may have destroyed Aziz's career. His crime was that he initiated a consensual sexual encounter. Instead of being held accountable for her passive aggressive behavior, the girl gets a pass.

Stories like Ansari's are scaring the hell out of men everywhere. Who wants to have sex under those conditions? It is too risky, and not just because of STDs.

The fallacy of MeToo is that most of what is being categorized as sexual misbehavior is merely the normal functioning of human beings. Leave it to the French to figure this out. A group of French women have composed an open letter to the Parisian newspaper *Le Monde* in which they expose MeToo for what it is. "Just like in the good old witch-hunt days," the women say, "what we are once again witnessing here is puritanism ... claiming to promote the liberation and protection of women, only to enslave them to a status of eternal victim and reduce them to defenseless preys of male chauvinist demons."

The argument behind MeToo is that women are helpless victims of powerful men. What a distortion of reality. When it comes to sexual behavior, women enjoy power over men all day long...and well into the night. A woman makes the decision about whether or not to go out with a man. The man, on the other hand, is stuck in the rejection seat. He has to assume the risk of asking her, while she gets to reject him. Men are putting their egos on the line every day. They suffer from the insecurity that results from knowing that a man can be shot down by any woman. This anxiety is terrifying for many men. Except in cases of forcible rape, the woman also decides if a couple will have sex. He has the burden of asking, but once again she makes the decision. Remove the Harvey Weinsteins from the equation and the idea that men abuse their power is a sadistic feminist concoction.

"We defend a freedom to *bother* as indispensable to sexual freedom," the French women continue. "Today we are educated enough to understand that sexual impulses are, by nature, offensive and primitive—but we are also able to tell the difference between an awkward attempt to pick someone up and what constitutes a sexual assault." The "frenzy" to accuse men of wrongdoing, the women suggest, helps those who believe in a "Victorian moral outlook." Men have been forced to resign from their jobs "when their only crime was to touch a woman's knee, try to steal a kiss, talk about 'intimate' things during a work meal, or send sexually-charged messages to women who did not return their interest."

Let me make something clear to adult women who are reading this article. If I touch your knee, it is not sexual abuse. If I tell you a dirty joke, it is not sexual abuse. If I attempt to kiss you, it is not sexual abuse. You are not a mannequin without means of resisting. You are a grown person with the option of telling me to get lost. And believe me, I will get lost unless my name is Harvey Weinstein. In that case, if you decide to tolerate my abusive behavior because you think it will further your career, please have the good taste to keep your mouth shut.

Here is the bottom line: If a man does something that offends you, give him the finger and get on with your life.

Clash Daily, January 30, 2018

Part Four: Issues

"The U.N. is worse than disaster. The U.N. creates conflicts. Look at the disgraceful U.N. Human Rights Council: It transmits norms which are harmful, anti-liberty and anti-Semitic, among other things. The world would be better off in its absence."

Charles Krauthammer

Chapter 10: Globalism and Climate Change

Why We Should Defund the UN

When I was a boy, we worshipped the United Nations. I remember taking the subway with my fourth grade class from Brooklyn into Manhattan, where we observed the countries of the world as they carried out the lofty founding purpose of the UN: to maintain peace and foster cooperation between nations. My classmates and I admired the lucky bureaucrats who worked in the beautiful glass building on the East River.

Today the UN has strayed from its original goals. In reaction, the US should defund the UN and kick their useless butts out of town. Let them set up shop in Riyadh or Beijing and see how they like it. There are many reasons in support of what I am suggesting, but for now let's stick to the two biggies: (1) The UN has become a pawn of the Islamic world; and (2) Self-serving UN bureaucrats are committed to a totalitarian globalist agenda that is diametrically opposed to US interests. Oh, I forgot a third reason: We can use the money.

Muslim states account for 18 of the 47 seats on the UN Human Rights Council. This Muslim bloc has been the driving force, says *cnsnews.com*, behind two key items on the Council's agenda: the campaign for anti-blasphemy laws and condemnations of Israel. Now it seems they have the support of UN Secretary General Antonio Guterres. Pamela Geller, author of *Stop the Islamization of America*, said Guterres "is a tool of the Organization of Islamic Cooperation, which has been running a years-long campaign against freedom of speech at the UN." Guterres has cited "Islamophobia" as the reason for increasing terrorism around the world. "One of the things that fuel terrorism," said Guterres, "is the expression in some parts of the world of Islamophobic feelings and Islamophobic policies and Islamophobic hate speeches."

WorldNetDaily argued that, "Guterres just gave a free pass to Islamic extremists to commit acts of terror throughout the world." It's a lot like blaming the victim, says Phillip Haney, author of *See Something Say Nothing*. "He's giving them an out. If they're not required to take any responsibility for their terrorism and can simply blame the Islamophobic Western world," says Haney, "it's only going to get worse."

John Guandolo, a former FBI counter-terrorism expert, said Islamophobia is the term Muslim leaders use to identify people who are guilty of the Islamic blasphemy laws. "This gives us the cherry on top of the argument for shutting down the United Nations and sending them back to their respective countries,"

Guandolo said. "It is an anti-American organization which is littered with spies and haters of liberty and justice."

"Guterres is doing the bidding of Islamic jihadists and is advancing Islamic conquest by silencing truthful speech about Islam," former Congresswoman Michelle Bachmann told WND. "No other religion enjoys such protection from criticism," Bachmann said. "Ironically, no other religion in current times has advanced more violence, carnage and bloodshed than Islam and yet Islam's gatekeepers demand their religion not be criticized. We need to recognize this is nothing more than a well-designed strategy to achieve Islamic conquest and the UN Secretary General is now the jihadist's advocate."

The other reason to dump the UN is the globalist agenda adopted by the left-wing bureaucrats on the banks of the East River. "The tin pot dictators at the UN are only interested in redistribution of wealth, population control, the buildup of megacities, and global governance under the UN aegis," says *canadafreepress.com.* UN globalists are pushing for open borders, penalties to stop global warming, and the destruction of capitalism.

The hysteria about global warming, says Senator James Inhofe, has been fueled by the UN's desire for global control. Global climate change policies, says Inhofe, would give the UN its own funding source and make it unaccountable to member nations. "The climate scare is not driven by climate scientists," agrees British political commentator Christopher Monckton. "It's not driven by any adverse circumstances in the world's weather. It is driven by a totalitarian political ideology." This ideology, says Monckton, is fostered by the unelected bureaucrats at the UN and EU.

Ottmar Edenhofer, German economist and UN official, admitted that global warming is a fiction created to camouflage the real intent of the UN—to redistribute the world's resources under the control of a totalitarian world government. "One has to free oneself from the illusion that international climate policy is environmental policy," argues Edenhofer. "Climate policy has almost nothing to do anymore with environmental protection. The next world climate summit is actually an economy summit during which the distribution of the world's resources will be negotiated."

Christiana Figueres, executive secretary of the UN's Framework Convention on Climate Change and the driving force behind the 2015 Paris Agreement, admitted that the goal of environmental activists is not to save the world from ecological calamity but to destroy capitalism. As reported in *Investor's Business Daily*, Figueres said, "This is the first time in the history of mankind that we are setting ourselves the task of intentionally, within a defined period of time, to change the economic development model that has been reigning for at least 150 years, since the Industrial Revolution." In case you don't understand what that means, UN bureaucrats—under the guise of responding to climate change—want to take what you have and give it to people in the less developed parts of the world.

Fox News reports that the US contributes approximately $8 billion per year to the United Nations and its affiliated organizations. Look at what we are getting in return—not a very good deal. Imagine how we could put that money to better use. Build a wall? End poverty? Rebuild the military? The UN doesn't do what its founders intended. Let's get rid of it.

Daily Caller, February 21, 2017

Global Warming—An Avalanche of Propaganda

It drives me nuts when somebody tries to pull the wool over my eyes. I hate being conned. That's why I am so disturbed by all the manufactured hysteria about climate change. The truth is clearly stated in my book, *In Lies We Trust*: "It cannot be claimed beyond a reasonable doubt that (a) global warming exists, or that (b) climate change is caused by human activities, or that (c) climate change is dangerous. I would like to remain open-minded on this issue but the more research I do, the more convinced I am that global warming is a giant hoax."

It used to be suicide to admit that you deny global warming. But now the media, which has supported the GW agenda lock, stock, and barrel, is reacting to an unexpected development: the president-elect and his nominee for EPA administrator are skeptical about climate change. It is finally acceptable to defy Al Gore and his gang of GW bullies. Articles agreeing with my position have been popping up all over the place.

"The oft-repeated claim that nearly all scientists demand that something dramatic be done to stop global warming is not true," a group of distinguished scientists revealed in the *Wall Street Journal*. "In fact, a large and growing number of distinguished scientists and engineers do not agree that drastic actions on global warming are needed." In support of this conclusion is the Global Warming Petition Project, in which 31,000 physicists and physical chemists contend that "there is no convincing scientific evidence that human release of carbon dioxide, methane, or other greenhouse gases is causing or will, in the foreseeable future, cause catastrophic heating of the Earth's atmosphere and disruption of the Earth's climate."

John Coleman, founder of the *Weather Channel*, is one of many skeptics who contradict the validity of GW science. "There is no significant man-made global warming at this time," said Coleman, "there has been none in the past and there is no reason to fear any in the future." But what about all the hysteria over carbon dioxide emissions? Says Coleman, "Efforts to prove the theory that carbon dioxide is a significant greenhouse gas and pollutant causing significant warming or weather effects have failed."

So why has the Obama Administration tried so hard to shove this nonsense down our throats? The answer is that alarmism over climate is being used to justify Obama's appetite for bigger government. "The government scares people into thinking that the end is nigh," *The Federalist Papers Project* explained, "and that the only way to turn it around is to cede control to the federal government and allow them to force their economy-killing policies on business."

Climate hysteria also reinforces Obama's globalist aspirations. "One has to free oneself from the illusion that international climate policy is environmental policy," confessed German economist and UN official Ottmar Edenhofer. "Climate policy has almost nothing to do anymore with environmental protection. The next world climate summit is actually an economy summit during which the distribution of the world's resources will be negotiated." Christiana Figueres, executive secretary of the UN's Framework Convention on Climate Change and the driving force behind the 2015 Paris Agreement, admitted that the goal of environmental activists is not to save the world from ecological calamity but to destroy capitalism. As reported in *Investor's Business Daily*, Figueres said, "This is the first time in the history of mankind that we are setting ourselves the task of intentionally, within a defined period of time, to change the economic development model that has been reigning for at least 150 years, since the Industrial Revolution."

In case you don't understand what that means, UN bureaucrats—under the guise of responding to climate change—want to take what you have and give it to people in the less developed parts of the world. That will play right into Obama's socialist dream of fundamentally transforming America. He thinks we have too much. Just as he wants to redistribute income from rich to poor domestically, Obama wants to do the same thing on a global scale even if it means crippling the US economy.

Climate Change Business Journal quantified the cost of proposed anti-GW measures at a whopping $1.5 trillion per year. That's $1.5 trillion to solve a non-existent problem. And what do we get for this waste of time, money, and effort? Danish environmentalist Bjorn Lomborg calculates that even if every nation in the world adheres to its climate change commitments by 2030, by the end of this century it will reduce the world's temperatures by a mere 0.048°C or 1/20th of a degree Celsius.

If you are still unconvinced that GW is a hoax, read Chapter Eight in my book where I describe how the US government, the UN, and the media have brainwashed us with an avalanche of propaganda. I lay out all the evidence that we are being conned. And that just makes me mad.

Daily Surge, January 3, 2017

Why Trump Must Reject the Paris Accord

President Trump is opting out of the Paris Accord on climate change. In response, this story was released by *The Associated Press*: "World powers lined up against U.S. President Donald Trump on climate change, reaffirming their support for international efforts to fight global warming." The image the media want to create is that US leadership is being abdicated by Trump. Democrats are wishing that their golden boy Obama occupied the Oval Office. He would show us how a real leader behaves. NOT. Sorry, children, but Obama messed things up two years ago. Fortunately, it is not too late for Trump to fix the mess. He can do so by recognizing the top three reasons for dumping the Paris Accord:

1. There is a preponderance of evidence that global warming is a giant hoax.
2. The Paris Accord is a disguised attempt by the UN and EU to redistribute economic resources and impose global governance.
3. The US can demonstrate its leadership by rejecting a bad deal.

Reason Number One: Global warming is a giant hoax. "The oft-repeated claim that nearly all scientists demand that something dramatic be done to stop global warming is not true," a group of distinguished scientists revealed in the *Wall Street Journal*. In support of this conclusion is the Global Warming Petition Project, in which 31,000 physicists and physical chemists contend that "there is no convincing scientific evidence that human release of carbon dioxide, methane, or other greenhouse gases is causing or will, in the foreseeable future, cause catastrophic heating of the Earth's atmosphere and disruption of the Earth's climate."

Climate change is recognized as a natural phenomenon. "Climate changes all the time," says physicist and Nobel laureate Ivar Giaever, "and it's nothing to do with global warming." John Coleman, founder of the *Weather Channel*, says, "There is no significant man-made global warming at this time, there has been none in the past, and there is no reason to fear any in the future."

Much of the hysteria about climate derives from Al Gore's 2006 film, *An Inconvenient Truth*. Gore made a series of ridiculous predictions: melting ice will cause a 20-foot rise in sea level "in the near future"; Arctic summer ice will "completely disappear" within five years; and we have until January 2016 to end our addiction to fossil fuels or *the world will come to an end*. Author Ben Shapiro nailed it when he observed that the environmental movement creates a crisis and then lies about it, falsifying evidence to convince people to give up their standard of living or we will all die.

Reason Number Two: The Paris Accord is a disguised attempt by the UN and EU to redistribute economic resources. If global warming is a hoax, why did Barack Obama try so hard to force this nonsense down our throats? The answer is that alarmism over climate was used by Obama to (a) justify his appetite for bigger government, and (b) reinforce his globalist aspirations. As exposed by Senator James Inhofe, the hysteria about climate change is fueled by the UN's desire for global control. "One has to free oneself from the illusion that international climate policy is environmental policy," confessed German economist and UN official Ottmar Edenhofer. "Climate policy has almost nothing to do anymore with environmental protection," he said. "The next world climate summit is actually an economy summit during which the distribution of the world's resources will be negotiated." In other words, the UN wants to take resources away from us and give them to third world countries.

Christiana Figueres, executive secretary of the UN's Framework Convention on Climate Change and the driving force behind the Paris Agreement, admitted that the goal of environmental activists is not to save the world from ecological calamity but to *destroy capitalism*. As reported in *Investor's Business Daily*, Figueres said, "This is the first time in the history of mankind that we are setting ourselves the task of intentionally to change the economic development model that has been reigning for at least 150 years, since the Industrial Revolution."

Reason Number Three: The Paris Accord is a bad deal and the US will demonstrate its leadership by rejecting it. The agreement does not provide penalties for non-compliance. Each signatory can decide what it wants to contribute—or not. "It's just worthless words," said renowned climate scientist James Hansen. "There is no action, just promises." China and India, two of the world's biggest polluters, are given a pass, but the agreement would impose an economic death-lock on the US.

Climate Change Business Journal quantified the cost of US acquiescence to the Paris Accord at a whopping $1.5 trillion per year. An expenditure of that magnitude would destroy the US economy. What would we get in return? MIT's Joint Program on the Science and Policy of Global Change projects that, even if every country followed through with its promises, the Paris Agreement would reduce warming by only 0.2 degrees Celsius by the year 2100. Danish environmentalist Bjorn Lomborg puts that figure at a mere 0.048 degrees Celsius or 1/20th of a degree. Hardly worth the effort.

European countries are proving their blindness on two major issues, immigration and climate change. President Trump is providing needed leadership in both areas by (a) not following Angela Merkel's suicidal policy of accepting unlimited numbers of Middle Eastern "refugees," and (b) acknowledging that the Paris Accord is a scam. By accepting the Paris Accord, we would be following—not leading—in order to appease the G20 nations. Appeasement has never worked. "Having other countries know that the U.S. President is resolute is valuable diplomatic currency," says *Fox News*, "not fecklessness." Someone has to stand up to the bullying by the UN and the EU. As usual, it will be up to us to push back against international shortsightedness. We are fortunate to have a president who understands this.

Daily Surge, July 11, 2017

Sorry Greta, Climate Crisis is UN-Sponsored Hysteria

Protestors from over 150 countries, led by battalions of brainwashed children, took part in demonstrations this week aiming to put pressure on governments and decision-makers to do more about what the protestors refer to as the "climate crisis." This is thought to be the largest climate action ever staged.

"We want to show the government that we aren't going to stand for inaction on climate change any more," said Beth, a student marcher from Wales in the UK. Greta Thunberg, the Swedish teenager/Joan of Arc-knockoff who has inspired school strikes for climate around the globe, warned, "This is only the beginning. Change is coming whether they like it or not."

The strikes are taking place ahead of the upcoming United Nations Climate Change Summit, staged by UN Secretary-General António Guterres in support of the 2015 Paris Agreement. There is only one problem with all of this furious activity. The so-called "climate crisis" is a massive hoax created by the UN to further its globalist ambitions by redistributing the world's resources. It has nothing to do with climate. The involvement of children as pawns in this game is strictly a political ploy and ought to be condemned.

The threat of horrific global warming was set in motion in 1972 by the UN-sponsored Intergovernmental Panel on Climate Change. Its conclusions were based on faulty science that has been refuted by thousands of scientists, including the 31,000 physicists and physical chemists of the Global Warming Petition Project. These experts contend that "there is no convincing scientific evidence that human release of carbon dioxide, methane, or other greenhouse gases is causing or will, in the foreseeable future, cause catastrophic heating of the Earth's atmosphere and disruption of the Earth's climate."

John Coleman, founder of the Weather Channel, is typical of the many "deniers" who contradict the validity of GW science. "There is no significant man-made global warming at this time," said Coleman, "there has been none in the past and there is no reason to fear any in the future." According to Nobel laureate Ivar Giaever, "climate changes all the time and it's nothing to do with global warming." MIT Professor Richard Lindzen refers to the global warming crowd as a cult. "As with any cult," Lindzen says, "once the mythology begins falling apart, instead of saying, oh, we were wrong, they get more and more fanatical."

We can thank opportunists like Al Gore and Barack Obama for spreading the hysteria that the ice will melt, the oceans will rise, and we will all die from heat exhaustion. Alarmism over climate was used to justify Obama's appetite for bigger government and to reinforce his globalist aspirations. "The government scares people into thinking that the end is nigh," *The Federalist Papers Project* explained, "and that the only way to turn it around is to cede control to the federal government and allow them to force their economy-killing policies on business."

The actual purpose of the UN climate strategy is out in the open. "One has to free oneself from the illusion that international climate policy is environmental policy," confessed German economist and UN official Ottmar Edenhofer. "Climate policy has almost nothing to do anymore with environmental protection. The next world climate summit is actually an economy summit during which the distribution of the world's resources will be negotiated."

Christiana Figueres, executive secretary of the UN's Framework Convention on Climate Change and the driving force behind the 2015 Paris Agreement, admitted that the goal of environmental activists is not to save the world from ecological calamity but to destroy capitalism. "This is the first time in the history of mankind," Figueres said, "that we are setting ourselves the task of intentionally, within a defined period of time, to change the economic development model that has been reigning for at least 150 years, since the Industrial Revolution."

In case you don't understand what that means, UN bureaucrats—under the guise of responding to climate change—want to take what you have and give it to people in the less developed parts of the world. The inevitable result: destruction of the US economy and standard of living. *Climate Change Business Journal* quantified the cost to the US of proposed anti-GW measures at a whopping $1.5 trillion per year. That's $1.5 trillion subtracted from our economy to solve a non-existent problem.

How do we justify crippling the US economy in pursuit of ghosts? What do we get for this waste of time, money, and effort? Danish environmentalist Bjorn Lomborg calculates that even if every nation in the world adheres to its climate change commitments by 2030, by the end of this century it will reduce the world's temperatures by a mere 0.048°C or 1/20th of a degree Celsius. In other words, the whole thing is a bad joke.

Author Ben Shapiro summed it up when he observed that the environmental movement creates a crisis and then lies about it, falsifying evidence to convince people to give up their standard of living or we will all die. The truth is just the opposite. If we allow special interest groups like the UN to have their way, it means economic suicide. We are fortunate that President Trump refuses to sacrifice the US economy on the counterfeit altar of climate change.

Reactionary Times, September 22, 2019

Chapter 11: Immigration

The Left's Immigration Fallacy

Barack Obama, Hillary Clinton, and their Democratic supporters have argued that we must accept millions of immigrants from Latin America and the Middle East because it is the "American Way." While it is true that we are a country of immigrants, the current situation is very different from anything we have faced in the past.

Historically, immigrants did not arrive on our shores with the stated intention of destroying our values and our civilization. On the contrary, they wanted to become Americanized. They wanted to speak English and to "fit in." They wanted their children to be Americans — not Italians or Irish or Germans. They could retain elements of their home culture, but their primary identification was American. And they expected to work hard to achieve that. They did not rely on entitlements and handouts from the government, because there weren't any.

Instead of assimilating and adopting American values as past immigrants did, today's immigrants want to impose their values on us. They want us to assimilate. Millions of Spanish-speaking immigrants want to flaunt the flag of their native country. They identify as Mexican or Salvadoran or Guatemalan. They expect everything to be translated for them into Spanish. They feel entitled to receive a treasure trove of benefits, while sending much of it back to the old country.

There is great irony when immigrants from south of the border take American citizenship as their right. As soon as the

Trump Administration announced plans to deport illegals, the Mexican government reacted defensively. "I want to say clearly and emphatically," said Mexican Foreign Minister Luis Videgaray, "that the government of Mexico and the Mexican people do not have to accept provisions that one government unilaterally wants to impose on the other." One would think that Mexico has liberal immigration laws. On the contrary, Mexico's draconian laws make ours seem extremely tolerant.

Mexico deems illegal immigration a felony punishable by up to two years in prison. Immigrants who are deported and attempt to re-enter can be jailed for up to 10 years. Visa violators can get six years. A Mexican who marries a foreigner with the sole objective of helping the foreigner to live in Mexico can get five years. In fact, Mexico has deported more illegal aliens than we have. From January to December, 2014, Mexico deported 107,199 Central American immigrants, while the US only deported 104,688 illegals. When a corrupt country like Mexico has the good sense to insist on the rule of law for its borders, why aren't we doing the same?

Muslim immigration takes the problem one step further. Muslim migrants want to supplant our democratic values with the murderous worldview of sharia. Wherever Islam gains a following, Muslims demand an end to human rights and the freedoms that are taken for granted in the West. All we have to do is look at what is happening right now in Europe. As a result of Muslim immigration in Europe, said British commentator Pat Condell, "our society is now measurably less safe and less civilized and the rights of women are effectively negotiable."

We cannot expect people from the Stone Age culture of the Middle East to be transported to New York or Chicago and automatically be assimilated. But that is the unreasonable expectation of the Left. Millions of Muslim immigrants in France,

Belgium, Germany, the UK, Holland, and Sweden refuse to integrate or accept Western values. "The experience of Western European countries which have ghettos and excluded localities shows that the integration of the Muslim community is practically impossible," said Czech President Milos Zeman. "Those coming here have no intention of adapting to our lifestyle," agreed Hungarian Prime Minister Viktor Orban.

Under Obama, the US lost sight of a basic truth in international relations: Every country has the right to protect its culture and its borders. Trump's intention is plain. He wants to enforce our existing immigration laws for the sake of law and order and to protect the homeland from terrorist incursions. We are a country of laws. When one law can be broken without consequences, it encourages disrespect for all laws. The Left, it seems, wants to suspend the rule of law when it suits their purpose. It doesn't take a genius to figure out that the Left supports mass immigration because the assumption is that most of them will vote Democratic. "If Americans won't vote for Democrats, then we'll import people who will."

Author and political commentator Monica Crowley reminds us that no foreigner has an inherent right to live in the US. When it comes to immigration, the needs of our citizens must come first. Washington's first responsibility is to Americans — our government is under no legal or moral obligation to anyone else.

American Thinker, June 20, 2018

Democrats' Objection to the Wall Constitutes Treason

That's right, I said it. The Democrats are guilty of treason. Just when I was beginning to think that eight years of trashing the republic during the Obama administration was as bad as it could get...it gets worse. This time, the Democrats have shown contempt for the primary function of government: protection of the homeland. By taking the side of illegal aliens against homeland security, the Democratic Party has adhered to our enemies.

The U.S. Constitution, Article III, states: *"Treason against the United States, shall consist only in levying War against them, or in adhering to their Enemies, giving them Aid and Comfort."* Jane Fonda gave aid and comfort to our enemy, North Vietnam. She was a traitor. The Democrats, by supporting sanctuary cities and refusing to pay for the wall, are giving aid and comfort to aliens who show contempt for our laws and sovereignty and who, by definition, are *enemies of the United States.*

What reasons do the Democrats give us when they refuse to allocate funds for the wall? The wall is immoral, Nancy Pelosi insists. A wall cannot be immoral. Neglecting the security and safety of American citizens is immoral. The wall is ineffective, says Alexandria Ocasio-Cortez. How can a wall be ineffective when it hasn't been built yet?

Then they say that walls don't work, even though history attests to the *irrefutable fact* that walls have worked for millennia. Walls are working today in Israel, for example, where a wall protects Israelis from enemy incursions. That is precisely what our wall will do—protect us from those who would do us harm: criminal gangs, terrorists, drug smugglers, human traffickers, people who take jobs from our citizens, and those who would force entry into the U.S. by breaking the law.

Next they fall back on the argument that a wall is too expensive. An ironic argument from a political party that loves to spend taxpayers' money with abandon. A lot of that money goes to foreign countries where it is used to build walls and protect their borders. If we can do it for them, why aren't we doing it for ourselves?

And we mustn't forget the argument that Trump is a racist. Anderson Cooper said on his CNN program that the president "is tired of so many black people coming into this country." Trump "seems to harbor racist feelings about people of color, from other parts of the world," said CNN's Jim Acosta. It is not racism to say we should admit people from functioning countries like Norway and not from dysfunctional "s***holes" like Haiti. We need immigrants who can contribute to our society, grow our economy, and assimilate into our culture. The U.S. government has an obligation to admit newcomers who will have a positive impact. That obligation is to our citizens and our citizens alone. We have no legal or moral obligation to anyone else.

Which brings up the "moral" argument in favor of open borders. The Left believes we have an obligation—based on "compassion"—to admit non-citizens who are suffering in s***hole countries. Who are we kidding? Most of the world is made up of s***hole countries. The residents of those countries would be crazy not to want to live in America. But if we open our borders to all who want to come, it will be impossible to accommodate the resulting tidal wave of immigrants. Try to imagine what would happen if we take in 100 million or 300 million or more "refugees." The economic and social costs of such a policy would tear us apart. Clearly we cannot afford to admit everyone who wants to come, nor is our government under any legal or moral obligation to satisfy the desires of the entire planet.

When all those arguments fail, we are told that Trump has "manufactured a crisis." During his address on January 8, the president clearly listed the reasons—*irrefutable facts*—why we have a crisis. If the situation on our southern border is not a crisis, what is? Once we accept that a crisis exists, there is no reasonable defense for opposing the wall. Why, then, do the Democrats persist in supporting open borders? There can be only one reason: importing Democratic voters.

The Democrat Party figured out that third-world immigrants will vote overwhelmingly for Democrats. Admitting them in droves will turn our country into a one-party system. No Republican will ever win a national election. This justification for mass immigration is an assault on our democratic values. Think about this: If a majority of illegals opted for Republicans, the Democrats would demand an immediate halt to immigration.

The ultimate irony is that before they recognized the potential for new voters, all the Democratic mouthpieces used to be against illegal immigration. In 2010, Chuck Schumer said, "People who enter the United States without our permission are illegal aliens and illegal aliens should not be treated the same as people who enter the United States legally." In 2005, Barack Obama said, "Those who enter the country illegally and those who employ them disrespect the rule of law and they are showing disregard for those who are following the law." In 1996, Nancy Pelosi said, "I agree with my colleagues that we must curb illegal immigration responsibly and effectively." As late as 2015, Hillary Clinton said, "I voted numerous times when I was a senator to spend money to build a barrier to try to prevent illegal immigrants from coming in."

Today the Democrats endorse open borders, the lottery system, chain migration, and non-enforcement of our existing laws because they hope that mass immigration will result in Democratic domination of the country. Democrats care about power, and that is all. The proof: Their political objective conflicts with national security interests. The only thing standing in their way is Donald J. Trump, who understands that our government's primary objective must be the protection of American interests. When one of our political parties cares more about illegal aliens than citizens, it is a direct violation of the public trust and Article III. If we have open borders, and if sanctuary cities and states can deliberately disregard federal statutes, we no longer have a country.

Clash Daily, January 11, 2019

Deal of the Century: The "Refugee" Gravy Train

Milton Friedman, the brilliant economist and Nobel Prize winner, said: "There's no such thing as a free lunch." Wrong, Milton, dead wrong. If you are a Muslim "refugee" and lucky enough to penetrate the borders of a bleeding-heart Western country, you can get a free lunch, dinner, and much, much more. When Muslims arrive in Europe, they are entitled to public housing or rent subsidies, food, "living allowance," clothing, health insurance, school supplies, daycare, child benefits, language lessons, and on and on.

"The refugees," says *National Review*, "or perhaps more accurate, economic migrants, choose Europe because of Europe's social safety net." *Investor's Business Daily* referred to the European welfare system as "the multiculturalist socialist paradise that the entire European Union affords Muslim immigrants." There is an element of irony here. "In Islamic law," according to *jihadwatch.org*, "non-Muslims have the duty to provide for the upkeep of Muslims." European nanny states are obliging.

"A staggering 80 percent of Muslims in Europe are on welfare," says *punchingbagpost.com*. "It's particularly bad in Belgium and the Netherlands, where each country's meager (about 5 percent) Muslim population consumes roughly 50 percent of the generous welfare budget." An estimated 40 percent of welfare outlays in Denmark go to the 5 percent of the population that is Muslim. Otto Schily, former German interior minister, admitted that, "seventy percent of the newcomers land on welfare the day of their arrival." In Sweden, immigrants are estimated at 1.5 million out of 10 million people and immigration is estimated to cost almost $14 billion per year. Enormous welfare expenditures are accompanied by high levels of unemployment. In Germany, only 2 million of 7.5 million foreigners were in the labor force.

Outrageous examples of welfare misuse abound. Take the Syrian refugee who was granted asylum in Germany along with his four wives and 23 children. He is reported by *breitbart.com* to be receiving 360,000 euros ($390,000) a year in benefits, sparking outrage among German citizens. An al-Qaeda woman arrested for plotting a terrorist attack in Brussels was receiving $1,100 a month in government unemployment benefits. In Denmark, 28 ISIS supporters each received $134 per day for two years. In the UK, Muslim men with more than one wife will receive extra benefits, reports the *Daily Mail*. Extra wives will be treated as single, allowing them to claim single person's benefits amounting to almost $400 a month for each wife in a polygamous household.

It has been suggested that the onslaught of Muslim immigrants is part of a terrorist plot. Consider this statement from *The Horn News*:

> *"It's not just bombs and bullets that Islamic terrorists are using to wage jihad against the West. It's the European welfare system. Radical Islamic leaders have revealed that part of their strategy of conquest is exploiting liberal immigration and welfare policies—leeching off the West's generous benefits while plotting to establish Islam as the dominant force in countries like Belgium, Denmark, and others."*

Meanwhile, the nanny states are discovering that they cannot bear the burden forever. As reported by *National Review*, Margot Wallström, Sweden's Social Democratic foreign minister, declared: "We cannot maintain a system where perhaps 190,000 people will arrive every year—in the long run, our system will collapse." As budgets dry up and right-wing parties gain ascendency, the European welfare spigot will shut down. Where will all the Muslim freeloaders go then? The land of the free and home of the brave. And the politically correct. And the naïve. Yes, coming to a town near you.

One of President Obama's primary goals, says *dailywire.com*, was to force the US to be more diverse and, particularly, less "Islamophobic." "A perfect way to do all that is to ramp up immigration from majority-Muslim countries, which by the end of his presidency he will have done to the tune of over one million green cards issued to Muslim migrants." In fiscal 2016, according to *Pew Research Center*, Muslims made up nearly half (46 percent) of refugee admissions to the US, a higher share than for Christians, who accounted for 44 percent of refugees admitted.

The gravy train, born in Europe, continues on this side of the Atlantic. In fiscal year 2013, Sen. Jeff Sessions found that 91.4 percent of Middle Eastern refugees received food stamps, 73.1 percent were on Medicaid or Refugee Medical Assistance and 68.3 percent were on cash welfare. But wait—President Trump has different plans for Muslim immigration. Memo to Milton Friedman: You may have been right after all—it could be the end of the free lunch.

Or is it? Where Muslim immigrants leave off, illegal immigrants from south of the border are filling in. The households of illegal immigrants receive an annual average of more than $1,000 in federal welfare benefits than do the households of non-immigrant recipients. According to the Center for Immigration Studies, the welfare payout to illegal immigrant households averages $5,692 yearly, compared with the average $4,431 welfare payout to non-immigrant households. Illegal immigrants are barred from directly receiving welfare, but may obtain it through their US-born children. Of course, this does not include healthcare, education, daycare, and other benefits.

Sorry, Milton, you missed the boat again. It looks like the free lunch has a life of its own.

Daily Surge, February 28, 2017

Immigration Hypocrisy: Mexico Can't Have It Both Ways

An interesting headline appeared on *Yahoo.com* this week: *"Mexico fumes over Trump immigration rules as US talks loom."* The Mexicans reacted defensively when the Trump administration announced plans to consider almost all illegal immigrants subject to deportation. Mexican Foreign Minister Luis Videgaray said his country would not accept the new US rules. "I want to say clearly and emphatically," Videgaray announced, "that the government of Mexico and the Mexican people do not have to accept provisions that one government unilaterally wants to impose on the other. We will not accept it, because there's no reason why we should, and because it is not in the interests of Mexico."

One would think Mexico has liberal immigration laws that make ours seem racist and xenophobic by comparison. Not even close. Get ready for an eye-opener. Here is a summary of Mexico's *General Law on Population*:

• Illegal immigration is a felony in Mexico. "A penalty of up to two years in prison and a fine of three hundred to five thousand pesos will be imposed on the foreigner who enters the country illegally." (Article 123)

• Immigrants who are deported and attempt to re-enter can be imprisoned for 10 years.

• Visa violators can be sentenced to six-year terms.

• Mexicans who help illegal immigrants are considered criminals. A Mexican who marries a foreigner with the sole objective of helping the foreigner live in the country is subject to up to five years in prison. (Article 127)

• Immigration officials must "ensure" that "immigrants will be useful elements for the country and that they have the necessary funds for their sustenance" and for their dependents. (Article 34)

• Foreigners may be barred from the country if their presence upsets "the equilibrium of the national demographics," when foreigners are deemed detrimental to "economic or national interests," when they do not behave like good citizens in their own country, when they have broken Mexican laws, and when "they are not found to be physically or mentally healthy." (Article 37)

• Federal, local and municipal police must cooperate with federal immigration authorities upon request, i.e., to assist in the arrests of illegal immigrants. (Article 73)

• Shipping and airline companies that bring undocumented foreigners into Mexico will be fined. (Article 132)

It is significant to recognize, as *American Thinker* points out, "there is no green card, no food stamps, or pathway to Mexican citizenship." And "while we invite illegal immigration with jobs, service in the US military, driver's licenses, and discounted college tuition denied US citizens from another state, Mexico slams the door," says *Investor's Business Daily*. In fact, Mexico has deported more illegal aliens than we have. From January to December, 2014, Mexico deported 107,199 Central American immigrants, while the US only deported 104,688 illegal immigrants. "How's that for irony?" said Ruben Navarrette on CNN. "It seems that Mexicans are no more keen on losing jobs to Guatemalans, Hondurans or Salvadorans than Americans are about losing them to Mexicans. There is no denying the hypocrisy of Mexicans who insist on a secure border to the south but would prefer a porous one to the north."

So what the hell is going on here? "Why is our great southern neighbor pushing us to water down our own immigration laws and policies," asks *humanevents.com*, "when its own immigration restrictions are the toughest on the continent?" What is fair for them ought to be fair for us. If we emulated Mexico's laws, they would denounce us as racists. Actually, Trump's policies are minor league compared to Mexico's.

One of Trump's campaign issues was his insistence that the US should not sell itself out in relationships with other nations. "We've made other countries rich while the wealth, strength and confidence of our country has disappeared over the horizon," Trump said in his inauguration speech. Under Obama, the US lost sight of a basic truth in international relations: Every country has the right to protect its borders. Trump's intention is plain. He wants to enforce our existing immigration laws for two reasons: for the sake of law and order (the president's job is to enforce the law, something that Obama never understood) and to protect the homeland from terrorist incursions. If Mexican politicians want to play hardball, I have no doubt Mr. Trump can show them how it's done.

Daily Surge, February 28, 2017

Democrats' Insane Immigration Demands Will Be the End of America

The fiasco known as U.S. immigration policy is an inch away from ending our republic. The Democratic Party endorses open borders, the lottery system, chain migration, and non-enforcement of our existing laws because mass immigration will result in Democratic domination of the country. The Republicans nearly let them get away with it. Enter Donald J. Trump. He showed courage and honesty by making immigration reform—a topic that no one else wanted to touch—the keystone of his presidential campaign.

Trump recognizes that either we are a country of laws or we are nothing. If millions of aliens are permitted to enter the U.S. illegally, and sanctuary cities and states can deliberately disregard federal statutes, we no longer have a country. The California attorney general has announced that he will prosecute companies that abide by federal immigration law. We witnessed something similar in 1963 when Governor George Wallace of Alabama tried to subvert federal civil rights laws. Wallace conceded defeat when President Kennedy intervened. If President Trump and Attorney General Sessions do not act swiftly and decisively in California, our children will inherit a non-country where no one will be safe from those who would show contempt for the rule of law.

The "bleeding heart" liberal position on immigration, embraced by the Democrats, is that anyone who wants to come to the U.S. should be allowed to do so. In other words, the Left believes we have an obligation—based on "compassion"—to admit non-citizens who are suffering in "s***hole" countries. Who are we kidding? Most of the world is made up of s***hole countries. The residents of those countries would be crazy not to want to live in America. But if we open our borders to all who want to come, it will be impossible to accommodate the resulting tidal wave of immigrants. The economic and social costs of such a policy would tear us apart. Clearly we cannot afford to admit everyone who wants to come, nor is our government under any legal or moral obligation to satisfy the desires of the entire planet.

So whom should we admit? The answer was articulated by White House spokesman Raj Shah: "Like other nations that have merit-based immigration," Shah said, "President Trump is fighting for permanent solutions that make our country stronger by welcoming those who can contribute to our society, grow our economy, and assimilate into our great nation." It is not racism to say we should admit people from functioning countries like Norway and not from dysfunctional s***holes like Haiti. The U.S. government has an obligation to admit newcomers who will have a positive impact on our country. That obligation is to our citizens and our citizens alone. We have no legal or moral obligation to anyone else.

We have laws on the books that would do the job if they were enforced. The Democratic Party and the mainstream media have made a mockery of those laws. Eleven million or more illegals have infiltrated our borders without permission, disappeared into the interior, and the government seems powerless to find them—let alone deport them. Most of them are unskilled and uneducated and must rely on government assistance. Most of them don't learn English and won't assimilate. They commit a disproportionate number of serious crimes, as exemplified by the Kate Steinle murder.

Ironically, we have videos from a few short years ago in which Bill Clinton and other prominent Democrats advocate strict enforcement of existing immigration laws. Not anymore. The Democrats figured out that third-world immigrants will vote overwhelmingly for Democrats. Admitting them in droves will turn our country into a one-party system. The Democratic position is purely political and has nothing to do with compassion. This justification for mass immigration is an assault on the democratic values that have been in place since the country was founded. Think about this: If a majority of illegals opted for Republicans, the Democrats would demand an immediate halt to immigration.

The Democrats have come up with another opportunistic ploy—the "dreamers." Their parents brought the dreamers here, illegally of course, and they grew up here. They demand citizenship and want to bring their parents back. We should "embrace" the dreamers, says Nancy Pelosi, and our nation should be "inspired" by them. Inspired by people who have shown contempt for our laws? Insane. The sensible answer to their demands is NO, because their parents *broke the law*. They should be blaming their parents—not U.S. immigration law—for their problems. The defining principle is that we have a right to decide who comes into our own country. That decision does not belong to people who protest our laws after coming here illegally. As Tucker Carlson pointed out, current illegal immigrants are determining the shape of future immigration. That is crazy.

Thanks to what is known as chain migration, each dreamer would of course want to bring in their mothers and fathers and sisters and brothers and cousins and so on. Mark Levin estimates that we have 3.6 million dreamers. Adding in their extended families would bring the total to more than 10 million. Combine that number with our 11 million or more "undocumented immigrants" and the potential total added to the Democratic voter rolls is staggering. Some states are issuing drivers licenses to "undocumented immigrants"—automatically making them "documented"—and then allowing them to vote. This will give the country over to the Democrats a lot faster without the necessity of conferring citizenship. Which brings up another sore point. The Democrats are against showing proof of identity at the polls. Their phony argument is that it will prevent blacks from voting. The real reason is that it gives Democrats another chance to influence elections using people who have no right to vote. If we are required to show an ID to get on an airplane, we can do the same when we vote.

In their quest for more and more power, Chuck Schumer, Nancy Pelosi, and their Democratic toadies want to take the U.S. down the road to destruction. We need to stop them by supporting Trump's effort to drain the swamp. And we need to do it now.

LifeZette, January 30, 2018

Identity Cards Are Dems' Frightening Solution to the Amnesty Crisis

The question over awarding citizenship to millions of illegal aliens and "dreamers" has emerged as one of the signal controversies plaguing the U.S. in the second decade of the 21st century. Those who believe in the rule of law, as this writer does, argue that giving citizenship to illegal immigrants violates federal immigration laws. If we permit one law to be ignored, all laws will be subject to individual whims and it will bring us closer to anarchy.

Liberals, on the other hand, insist that citizenship should be awarded to all people who entered the country illegally. It is no secret by now that the Democratic Party is in favor of open borders not for reasons of compassion but in order to swell the voting rolls. Their assumption is that Hispanic immigrants will vote overwhelmingly for Democratic candidates. If millions of illegal immigrants are granted citizenship, the Democrats will own the country because no Republican will ever be elected to major national office. The big question for the Democratic Party is: How do we get all these undocumented people into the voting booths?

Democratic Mayor Rahm Emanuel of Chicago is pointing the way. He plans to offer an identity card—known as the CityKey—to anyone who applies, including people who are in the country illegally and who are labeled as "undocumented immigrants." The card will contain the bearer's photo, date of birth, and residence address but no reference to citizenship status. People who previously were "undocumented" will automatically become "documented." To encourage illegals to use the program, Chicago will not maintain a record of the background information applicants provide to establish their home addresses. How convenient. Federal immigration agents will not be able to track them down.

Chicago officials have cited the example of San Francisco, another illegal "sanctuary" jurisdiction that has issued a similar identity card to 30,000 people since 2009. To receive a card in the city by the bay, all an illegal alien has to do is show a foreign passport, a foreign driver's license, a utility bill, an employment pay stub, or written verification from a homeless shelter. As in Chicago, no record is kept of the cardholder's address.

A majority of Chicago's aldermen voted in favor of the CityKey program. One alderman said—with a straight face—that the new ID card is a good idea because it will eliminate the need for illegals to break the law by obtaining fake IDs as they do now. According to the *Chicago Tribune*, the CityKey "is viewed in City Hall circles as a way for Emanuel to boost his standing with Hispanic voters and immigrant rights supporters as he preps a 2019 re-election bid."

The Illinois Elections Code charges the Chicago Board of Elections to accept current, valid photo identification cards as proof of identity and residency. In other words, the CityKey will be a valid ID for anyone attempting to vote. The City of Chicago will be enabling non-citizens to vote in violation of federal law. Under Illinois state law, city officials claim, voters are not required to prove they are American citizens. All a person needs to do is say "I am a citizen" and they can vote. Mayor Emanuel appears unconcerned that he may be abetting voter fraud.

The ramifications of the CityKey go way beyond local politics. Chicago and San Francisco are not alone in making it easier for illegals to vote. According to the National Conference of State Legislatures, 12 states and the District of Columbia have enacted laws to enable "unauthorized immigrants" to obtain a driver's license. In 34 states, a valid driver's license is all you need to vote. You may vote in 16 states without showing any identification at all.

Can you see where this is heading? The plan of the Democratic Party is to use dubious forms of ID in order to give voting rights to illegals. If they can get away with this subterfuge, the issue of whether we should award citizenship to millions of illegal immigrants will become irrelevant. Congress won't have to vote on it and the president will be spared the trouble of alienating his base. We won't have to give anyone citizenship because the rights and privileges that normally are reserved for citizens will be available to anyone with a phony ID. The value of U.S. citizenship will dwindle to zero. Why aspire to citizenship when all the perks are available without it?

In such a scenario, we can expect untold millions to cross our borders illegally with the assurance that they will be able to vote in our elections and receive free healthcare, education for their children, welfare payments, unemployment benefits, social security, etc. Unethical politicians are selling our beloved country and the rule of law down the river. I hope I never live to see it.

LifeZette, March 4, 2018

Chapter 12: Islam

The Islamophobia Scam

Our effort to defend against Islamic terrorism has been cut off at the knees by a thought crime known as *Islamophobia*: a dislike of, criticism of, or prejudice against Islam or Muslims. Where did Islamophobia come from? "Islamic law," observes author and activist Pamela Geller, "considers any critical examination of Islam to be blasphemous and subject to the death penalty." The term Islamophobia was invented in the 1990s by a front group of the Muslim Brotherhood in order to export Islamic blasphemy laws to the West. Muslim writer Abdur-Rahman Muhammad reveals the original intent behind the concept: "This loathsome term is nothing more than a thought-terminating cliché conceived in the bowels of Muslim think tanks for the purpose of beating down critics."

Islamophobia is classic political correctness. You don't have to deal with the substance of arguments against Islamic extremism. All you have to do is label critics a cluster of "Islamophobes." If this lie prevails, we become infinitely more vulnerable to terrorism and the negative impact of Islam because we are afraid to talk about them. As a manipulation, it has been highly effective.

Here is an example of what is described as Islamophobia: British author and journalist Douglas Murray said, "Less Islam in general is a good thing. It is not worth continuing to risk our own security simply in order to try to be politically correct." Murray echoes the sentiment succinctly expressed by Mark Steyn, author of the prophetic *America Alone*: "The choice is liberty or mass Muslim immigration." Steyn has warned about the correlation between large numbers of Muslim immigrants and the proliferation of terrorist attacks against Western values. Germany, England and France have opened their borders to hordes of Muslim immigrants and the reward has been disruption of their societies. Poland and the Czech Republic "have very few Muslims so they don't have terrorism," notes Steyn.

Murray has been vilified as an Islamophobe by Miqdaad Versi of the Muslim Council of Britain on the grounds that Murray and those like him are spreading hate. Anyone who criticizes Islam, says Versi, is "spreading hate" and is a "hate preacher." Islamophobia is used in this way to defame and silence anyone who tries to combat the problem of Islamic terrorism. The UK and other European countries have bought into this nonsense by criminalizing "hate speech." Islam has won its first significant battle against Western values with the suicidal collaboration of Western governments.

Versi and his Muslim apologists have it all backwards. Murray is not spreading hate—he is criticizing the hateful ideology and acts of terror that are the calling cards of Islam. When you denounce Islam for its intolerance, misogyny, and glorification of violence, that does not make you a spreader of hate. It makes you a critic of the most hateful ideology on the planet. The question is, do we support Murray's critique as an expression of free speech? In a free society, the answer must be a resounding YES.

In the US, the thrust of the Islamophobia strategy is to (a) accuse Americans of harboring a deep prejudice against Muslims, (b) convince the public that, as a result, Muslims are disproportionately targeted by perpetrators of hate crimes and acts of discrimination, and (c) suppress any and all criticism of

Islam and Muslims. "This sense of victimization has now reached a point that many rank-and-file Muslims genuinely believe that they are a persecuted and oppressed group," says Abdur-Rahman Muhammad. In reality, FBI data on hate crimes show that the incidence of anti-Muslim abuses in the US has actually declined since 9/11 and that anti-Islamic hate crimes constitute a small fraction of overall religious hate crimes. In 2006, for example, 66 percent of religiously motivated attacks in the US were against Jews and only 11 percent targeted Muslims. Even in the immediate aftermath of 9/11, there was virtually no violent backlash against Muslims in the US.

Salman Rushdie, the author who was sentenced to death by Muslim clerics, criticized the use of Islamophobia by saying that "ideas cannot be ring-fenced just because they claim to have this or that fictional sky god on their side. It is right to feel phobia towards such matters. To feel aversion towards such a force is not bigotry. It is the only possible response to the horror of events." The late author Christopher Hitchens reminded us that the language of the First Amendment "was designed to protect criticism of religion." Referring to Islamophobia as "religious bullying," Hitchens said, "We have to hear propaganda in the Muslim world telling children to kill Jews, Christians, and Hindus. That homosexuals should be stoned. And we have to claim not to be offended."

Muslims have become a special protected class. You can say nasty things about Christians and Jews, but if you criticize Muslims, you are accused of spreading hate. Thanks to the fear of Islamophobia, our great institutions of learning have been intimidated into trashing the First Amendment. *Yale University Press* has declined to publish the Danish cartoons that were declared offensive to Muslims. At the University of Minnesota, an attempt to recognize the 9/11 terrorist attacks was blocked because protesting students argued that the memorial could fuel Islamophobia. Brandeis University planned to award an honorary degree to Ayaan Hirsi Ali, an outspoken critic of Islam. When the university's president received a letter from the Council on American-Islamic Relations calling Hirsi Ali a "notorious Islamophobe," Brandeis reversed course and decided not to award a degree. I suppose Brandeis feels it is okay to stifle free speech now that Yale has set the precedent.

"The political correctness that has metastasized in American culture requires that no one speak ill of Islam or say anything that might stigmatize or *other-ize* a Muslim in any way," says journalist Matthew Vadum. "All Americans must think and say only nice things about Islam," he adds. "To object to this kind of politically correct censorship is not to make the gross generalization that Muslims are bad people, but it is to say that people have the right to criticize."

The Islamophobia scam is insidious because it shuts down the most important of American values, freedom of speech. We must not allow our core values to be trampled upon by a barbaric seventh-century ideology. The really scary news: One group in the US actually approves of the Islamophobia scam. According to a poll by Wenzel Strategies, 58 percent of Muslim-Americans believe criticism of Islam is not protected free speech under the First Amendment. "To learn who rules over you," said Voltaire, "simply find out who you are not allowed to criticize."

Daily Caller, August 2, 2017

Islamic Immigration: A Package Deal

Once again, I hear the old chorus of apologists for Islam as they talk down to us, preaching that compassion justifies mass Muslim immigration into the US. Actress Angelina Jolie justifies it by calling Islam a "beautiful religion." President Obama called it the "religion of peace." What the hell is wrong with these people? Nothing is beautiful or peaceful about a religion that demands death for apostates, nonbelievers, and homosexuals; intolerance of other faiths; and the medieval subjugation of women and children. Sorry, Angelina. Murder, intolerance, and misogyny are not the hallmarks of a beautiful religion.

Yet the apologists argue that accepting immigrants is the American way. That we are a nation of immigrants. That the president's ban on immigration from dysfunctional Middle Eastern countries is contrary to America's noblest traditions. That by closing the door to Muslims, we are violating freedom of religion. While it is true that we are a country of immigrants, the current situation is very different from anything we have faced in the past.

Historically, immigrants did not arrive on our shores with the stated intention of destroying our values and our civilization. On the contrary, they wanted to become Americanized. They wanted to speak English and to "fit in." They wanted their children to be American. None of this applies to Muslim immigration. Instead of assimilating and adopting American values as past immigrants did, Muslim immigrants want to impose their values on us. They want us to assimilate. All we have to do is look at what is happening right now in Western Europe as their societies are under attack from millions of Muslim immigrants who refuse to integrate or accept Western values.

The freedom of religion argument is refuted by a single question: Is Islam a religion or an ideology? My view is that Islam is a totalitarian political ideology cloaked in the disguise of a religion, which allows it to get away with murder—literally. "We have to stop pretending that Islam is a religion," says Dutch parliamentarian Geert Wilders. "A free society should not grant freedom to those who want to destroy it." When the power centers of the Islamic world cite the Quran to advocate *and in fact demand* the brutal murder of anyone whose behavior is deemed *offensive*—a code word for anyone who denies the core beliefs of Islam—then we are no longer dealing with a religion. Now what we have is a murder cult, and there is nothing in the Bill of Rights that supports this. "Let's not be politically correct about it," says former Muslim Ayaan Hirsi Ali, "Islam is a destructive, nihilistic cult of death. It legitimates murder."

When opponents of a mega-mosque in Tennessee claimed that Islam is not a religion, the Muslim-appeasing Obama administration intervened to insist that Islam is entitled to First Amendment protections. This kind of partisan support from our politicians has come in spite of numerous radical imams who openly advocate the violent overthrow of the US government. So let me adjust my argument ever so slightly. Assuming—purely for argument's sake—that Islam is a religion, we must recognize that it differs from other world religions in its dual roles as both religion and aggressive political force. Only in Islam is the line blurred between religious dogma and statism.

The Founding Fathers knew from personal experience and European history that merging politics and religion would lead to the destruction of the basic freedoms embodied in the First Amendment. Separating the two was a novel concept that made America unique. Islam is incompatible with American values for many reasons, not the least of which is that there is *no separation of church and state in Islam.* Author Shahi Hamid explains that the difference between Christianity and Islam regarding the state has to do with each religion's central figure:

> *"Unlike Jesus, Muhammad was both prophet and politician. And more than just any politician, he was a state-builder as well as a head of state. Not only were the religious and political functions intertwined in the person of Muhammad, they were meant to be intertwined."*

Islam's objective is a combination of political power and religious glory to be realized under a worldwide Muslim caliphate. This crucial distinction marks Islam as a special case. The obedient Muslim is ordered by his holy book to conquer and subdue people of other religions until they are in a full state of submission. The Quran is clear that Muslims will never be satisfied until all people submit to the tenets of Islam and the laws of sharia. If we accept the religion of Islam into our country, we are also accepting its totalitarian political ideology as manifested by murder, intolerance, and misogyny. We don't get to choose. Like it or not, one comes with the other. It's a package deal.

Disturbed European politicians like Angela Merkel have lied to their constituencies by pretending that the religion will come without the political ramifications. The result of their policies is the destruction of Europe as we know it. Germany, France, Holland, the UK, Sweden, and Belgium are being torn apart by violence and sexual assault on a massive scale. "Our society is now measurably less safe and less civilized and the rights of women are effectively negotiable," said British political commentator Pat Condell. "We need to stop the Muslim invasion," he advised, "and if you think that sounds harsh the alternative is a million times worse."

Whether we admit it or not, Islam has been waging a war against our civilization for 1,400 years. "How hard is it to understand that radical Islamic jihadis have declared war on the West?" asks Raheel Raza, founding member of the Muslim Reform Movement. It is naïve to think that the US is exempt. "Muslims are working in the United States now to make sure that Islam dominates by destroying our Constitutional freedoms," says author Pamela Geller. "How do I know that? Because they've told us."

Americans have been indoctrinated by the Left to ignore this clear and present danger. We are so intellectually weak that, rather than speak the truth, we let them get away with labeling us "Islamophobic." We vehemently deny the accusation and support the Left's position, certain that we have the moral high ground. How can we fall for such simplistic nonsense? Is the American public so gullible? As in Europe, the public refuses to believe that Islamophobia is *the only justifiable response* to Islamic aggression. We have become our own worst enemy.

The European tragedy is one step away from happening here. Our elected representatives have been trying to push this vile deceit on you and me. The only politician who recognizes and acknowledges the threat is the president. For this reason alone, Donald Trump may go down in history as the man who saved America.

Daily Surge, September 7, 2017

What Should We Do About Islam?

The United States is in the midst of a serious quandary: What should our position be on the subject of Islam and Islamic terrorism? Unfortunately, our government—which should be clarifying our intentions—has created a great deal of confusion. We do not have a coherent strategy for Islam and the Middle East.

In spite of the horror of 9/11 and more than 28,000 terrorist attacks from Islamic sources since 9/11, President Obama insists on referring to Islam as a religion of peace. He is reluctant to commit our resources in combatting Islamic extremism abroad and the potential for terrorism at home. As former CIA officer and political strategist Clare Lopez has pointed out, Obama's policies with respect to the Islamic world have favored our enemies and undermined our allies. It is therefore reasonable to ask the question: Whose side is he on?

The liberal view supports the president. While a small percentage of Muslims are radicalized, the left alleges, the majority are peace-loving people who embrace values that are compatible with ours. Last night, I watched a TV interview with college students furious at anyone who criticizes Islam. "We are not at war with Islam," they said. "Muslims are doctors and lawyers and loyal Americans." These students, and many liberals, are offended by President-elect Trump's stated intention to close the borders to Muslim immigrants.

I do not share the liberal viewpoint. Islam is not a religion as we define the word. Islam is a totalitarian political ideology, masquerading as a religion, whose aim is global domination. The theocratic Islamic state is no different from Nazi Germany, Stalinist Russia, or Maoist China in its demand for total control over the individual. Mainstream Islam's holy book, the Quran, demands that all other worldviews are to be exterminated. Non-Muslims are to be converted or killed, apostates are to be killed, homosexuals are to be killed, and women are to be completely subjugated. "Let's not be politically correct about it," said activist and former Muslim Ayaan Hirsi Ali. "Violence is inherent in Islam. It's a destructive, nihilistic cult of death. It legitimates murder." It is about time we recognized the truth that Islam is, in the words of Clare Lopez, "a supremacist genocidal ideology" under which murder, rape, and looting are "divinely sanctioned—commanded by Allah!"

Islamic values represent an absolute contradiction to ours. The two systems cannot coexist. Wherever Islam gains a following—take a look at Europe—Muslims demand an end to human rights and the freedoms that are taken for granted in the West. We can't have it both ways. "For a democracy that believes in freedom, peace, and prosperity," said General James Mattis, "the idea that this level of evil can exist is incompatible with our view of what we would like to see as we turn over this world to our children."

The threat from Islam is not new. We have been on the receiving end of what is often called "political Islam" since the founding of our republic. More than 200 years ago, the U.S. was forced to land marines in North Africa by Muslim terrorists who were not very different from those we face today. Islam's bigoted dogma is being spread throughout the U.S. by mosques and religious schools funded by Saudi Arabia, Iran, and Qatar. Their openly acknowledged intention is to replace the moral and legal foundations of the U.S. with the medieval code of Islam, Sharia.

Without compromising my position, I recognize that many Muslims worldwide do not practice the ideologically destructive aspects of their so-called religion. They identify as Muslim for ethnic and sociological reasons. My response is that these "moderate" Muslims have become irrelevant because they are allowing the hardliners to run the show. Islam is in need of reform. In the West, we used to burn people at the stake for disagreeing with church doctrine. Islam is in dire need of a series of reforms comparable to those instituted by Christianity in the sixteenth through the eighteenth centuries. Until that reformation occurs, we have a responsibility to defend our values from the encroaching threat posed by people who hate everything we stand for.

Daily Surge, December 7, 2016

Long-Overdue Response to Islamic Terror

Our new president has issued an executive order to close the US to immigrants from Iraq, Syria, Iran, Sudan, Libya, Somalia, and Yemen. His purpose is to protect us from Islamic terrorists who originate in those countries. This is a complete turnaround from Obama's do-nothing policy. Obama would not even acknowledge the threat from Islamic terrorism. He forbade government employees and the military from using words and phrases such as "Islamic terrorism," "jihad," and "Allah." As a direct result, we have been more vulnerable to attack. It has been suggested that the terror nightmare in Orlando could have been prevented if Obama had not censored the DHS from acknowledging the existence of a threat.

The argument against Trump's executive order, according to Ryan Crocker, former US ambassador to Iraq and Afghanistan, is that it will "confirm to the world that we are anti-Muslim." Madeline Albright, former secretary of state, seems to agree. She has expressed her solidarity with Muslims who, she believes, are being discriminated against because of their religion. Albright is ready to register as a Muslim if such registration becomes policy.

The fallacy of the dissenting arguments is that they have it completely backwards. Trump's executive order does not demonstrate that the US is anti-Muslim or that we discriminate based on religion, but rather demonstrates that we recognize a simple fact: *Islam is anti-US*. Not only are the teachings of mainstream Islam at odds with American values, the doctrine of jihad demands that Muslims should attack and destroy Western society. It is not bigotry to criticize Islam on the grounds that it is a bigoted ideology. When you accuse someone of being bigoted, that does not make you a bigot. It makes you an accuser. The question is whether your accusation is justified.

So is it correct to accuse Islam of being a bigoted political ideology that seeks the destruction of our values and political institutions? Islam is a religion of intolerance, preaching openly from its holy book against the rights of women, homosexuals, Christians, Jews, and anyone who deviates from the true religion. "How hard is it to understand that radical Islamic jihadis have declared war on the West?" asks Raheel Raza, president of the Council for Muslims Facing Tomorrow and founding member of the Muslim Reform Movement. "In simple English," she says, "this means: *they will find you and kill you wherever and whenever they can.*" Former Muslim Ayaan Hirsi Ali, in her book, *Heretic*, writes: "It is foolish to insist, as our leaders habitually do, that the violent acts of radical Islamists can be divorced from the religious ideals that inspire them. Let's not be politically correct about it. Islam is a destructive, nihilistic cult of death." In a similar vein, Dutch parliamentarian Geert Wilders said, "We have to stop pretending that Islam is a religion. Islam is a totalitarian ideology that aims to conquer the West. A free society should not grant freedom to those who want to destroy it."

Before criticizing Trump's motives, it is instructive to examine the language he uses in his executive order:

> *In order to protect Americans, we must ensure that those admitted to this country do not bear hostile attitudes toward our country and its founding principles. We cannot, and should not, admit into our country those who do not support the U.S. Constitution, or those who would place violent religious edicts over American law. In addition, the United States should not admit those who engage in acts of bigotry and hatred (including "honor" killings, other forms of violence against women, or the persecution of those who*

practice other religions) or those who would oppress members of one race, one gender, or sexual orientation.

The president is doing his job by protecting us from those who would do us harm. Instead of being blindsided by the religious discrimination argument, we need to recognize the threat Islam poses to this country. Don't believe it? Just look at what is taking place in Europe because of misguided leftist values that have opened the floodgates to Muslim terrorists. "The experience of Western European countries," said Czech president Milos Zeman, "shows that the integration of the Muslim community is practically impossible."

"Our society is now measurably less safe and less civilized and the rights of women are effectively negotiable," said British political commentator Pat Condell about the result of Muslim immigration. We need to stop the Muslim invasion, he advised, "and if you think that sounds harsh the alternative is a million times worse."

Daily Surge, January 27, 2017

The Democrats Will Get Us All Killed

Eight innocent civilians were murdered this week on the streets of New York City by a man from Uzbekistan yelling "Allahu akbar." Yet listening to Democratic politicians such as Governor Cuomo, Mayor De Blasio, and Senator Schumer, one would conclude that Islamic terrorism had nothing to do with it. The overriding concern of Democrats is to avoid an anti-Muslim backlash and to hell with the security of our citizens. According to the governor, there was no evidence of Islamic terror and the killer—*who asked to hang an ISIS flag in his hospital room*—was a "lone wolf." To paraphrase a comment by talk show host Mark Levin, these politically correct Democratic politicians could get us all killed.

For eight years, I listened to President Obama try to convince Americans that they have nothing to fear from Islamic terrorism. In fact, Obama insisted that there is no such thing as Islamic terrorism. Under his orders, government employees and the military were forbidden to use words and phrases such as *Islamic terrorism*, *jihad*, and *Allah*. As a direct result, we have been more vulnerable to attack. It has been suggested that the terror nightmare in Orlando could have been prevented if Obama had not censored the Department of Homeland Security from acknowledging the existence of a threat. It turns out that this week's Uzbek butcher frequented a mosque that was under surveillance by the New York Police Department's excellent counterterrorism unit. Unfortunately for this week's victims, that special unit could not prevent their murders because it was shut down in 2014 on the orders of Mayor De Blasio. The president did it, so the mayor of our largest city—another Democratic left-wing ideologue—figured it was a good idea to follow suit.

Philip Haney and other former DHS officials have revealed that Obama deliberately ordered the destruction of anti-terrorist intelligence that had been collected for years. How is it possible that an American president was capable of doing something so contemptuous of the country's welfare? "I can no longer be silent," Haney testified, "about the dangerous state of America's counter-terror strategy, our leaders' willingness to compromise the security of citizens for the ideological rigidity of political correctness—and, consequently, our vulnerability to devastating, mass-casualty attack."

The worst part of America's counter-terror strategy can be found in our self-destructive immigration policies. The perpetrator of the latest atrocity came into this country thanks to the Diversity Visa Program, which offers a lottery for people from countries with few immigrants in America. A lottery? That's correct, our Congress has made it possible for potential terrorists to enter the US if they win a lottery. Remember—we elected the people who voted for this. Yet when Donald Trump wants to fix the current policies, his immigration bans are thwarted by rogue judges and he is excoriated by the Left as a racist and bigot.

It is not bigotry to recognize that the obedient Muslim is ordered by his holy book to conquer and subdue people of other religions until they are in a full state of submission. The Quran is clear that violence and murder are required until all people submit to the tenets of Islam and the laws of sharia. If we accept the religion of Islam into our country, we are also accepting its totalitarian political ideology as manifested by murder, intolerance, and misogyny. We don't get to choose. Like it or not, one comes with the other. It's a package deal.

Daniel Horowitz, senior editor of *Conservative Review*, agrees: "Whenever we admit fervent Sharia-believing Muslims from the Middle East and they commit terror attacks on our soil, we never have a family discussion over suicidal immigration policies. How many people must die before it becomes in vogue to speak that truth—that when you bring the Middle East to your shores ... you bring the Middle East to your shores." Mark Levin is but one of many who have voiced frustration with leftist politicians who attack individuals for acknowledging that the Muslim community in America includes a significant group of radicals that seek to damage the United States from within.

In complete denial of these facts, Democrats are worried that protecting our citizens from attack will result in a backlash against peaceful American Muslims. This all began with Obama's attorney general, Loretta Lynch, who responded to the San Bernardino terrorist attack by revealing that her "greatest fear" was the rise of anti-Muslim rhetoric. Where did she come up with this? Even after 9/11, there was no anti-Muslim backlash. Hate crimes against Muslims actually have declined since 9/11 and constitute only a small fraction of overall hate crimes. Today's Democrats are following the precedent set by the Obama administration as they refuse to accept the danger we face from Islamic terrorism.

I can think of many reasons not to vote for Democrats, but the most compelling justification has been exposed this week by their spineless reaction to the latest in a long line of atrocities committed in the name of an omniscient being from the desert. Let's get rid of these left-leaning ideologues before they get us all killed.

Daily Surge, November 3, 2017

Some of My Best Friends Are Muslims: A Dangerous Argument

Comedian and magician Penn Jillette has an intriguing post on *YouTube* in which he explains his attitude about Islamophobia. He leads off with this pronouncement: "You are allowed to hate ideas; you are not allowed to hate people for their ideas." In other words, an ideology should be separated from the proponents of that ideology. We can criticize Islam, he argues, but we must not criticize Muslims as individuals. "Islamophobia is not racism," says Jillette. "Saying anything against Muslims is."

Following Jillette's logic, we are justified in despising the ideology of Nazism but we ought not to condemn individual Nazis. Jillette would give Hitler a pass—he wasn't such a bad fellow, it was only the Nazi ideology that stunk. No thank you, Mr. Gillette. When someone tells me that he is a Nazi, I must condemn that person because of his belief in a barbaric ideology. If a person advocates the ideology of Islam—which includes murder, intolerance, and misogyny—that person must be held to account. Calling these people out for their vile beliefs is not racism.

Jillette, obviously an intelligent and thoughtful person, has fallen into the trap that I call, "Some of my best friends are Muslims." This is a trap because it excuses people who subscribe to the tenets of Islam from responsibility for their beliefs. No ideology exists in a vacuum. An ideology exists because people believe in it. Separating believers from their ideology is a logical fallacy. The example I give in two of my books is Thuggee, a 19th century Indian religious cult based on worship of the Hindu goddess Kali. Adherents of Thuggee were called upon to strangle as many victims as possible in the name of their ideology.

Thuggee was responsible for 30,000 murders a year in India until the British finally put a stop to it. We cannot separate the individual "thug" from the ideology of his religion. Yet that is precisely what Jillette is suggesting.

In case you think comparing Islam to Thuggee is out of proportion, consider this quote from *Healthy Magazine*: "In just over 1,400 years, Muslims have slaughtered more than 270 million non-Muslims—and that's just the low estimation. How many more people must be killed at the hands of Muslims before we recognize that their motivation comes from their religion's commands to kill?"

Mr. Jillette believes that although the tenets of Islam may be reprehensible, his Muslim friends are peaceful and caring. "Muslims really need our help," he says. "We must love them, we must embrace them, even if they believe things we know are wrong." Jillette contradicts himself when he admits that Muslims believe "things we know are wrong." When someone says he wants to kill me because I do not "submit" to Islam, I am not going to turn the other cheek. I don't have the luxury of separating that person from his ideology. People who threaten to kill me are my enemies. When they try to deflect my justifiable ire by calling me an Islamophobe, that is a self-serving attempt to avoid taking responsibility for their obedience to a barbaric, seventh-century cult.

The argument usually given in support of "Some of my best friends are Muslims" is that millions of Muslims do not accept the hateful elements of Islam and are not terrorists. In response, I would suggest that any Muslim who disregards the basic tenets of the religion—killing non-believers, apostates, and homosexuals; subjugation of women; intolerance of other religions—is not a Muslim. Worldwide, we have millions who call themselves Muslims but who really are not Muslims. They may identify as Muslim only for ethnic or social reasons. Similarly, many self-described Catholics and Jews do not follow their religion, but think of themselves as Catholic or Jew because their family practiced that religion. Jillette cites the example of a Pakistani-American, raised as a Muslim, who is afraid to announce his atheism because there are Muslims out there who would without a doubt try to kill him for the sin of apostasy.

But regardless of whether they believe or don't believe, the Muslims-in-name-only must be held accountable because their passive behavior enables the worst aspects of the Islamic ideology. Their silence is evidence of complicity. Unfortunately, we don't have enough ex-Muslims—Ayaan Hirsi Ali, for example—who are outspoken in their rejection of Islam.

Jillette's "Some of my best friends are Muslims" approach is dangerous because it inhibits our defense against the jihadists and their assault upon Western civilization. Giving a pass to Muslims promotes tolerance for an intolerant Stone Age political ideology that wants to replace the Bill of Rights and the Constitution with sharia. We have a right and a responsibility to demand that immigrants to this country accept the values that our ancestors fought and died for. Islamic values represent an absolute contradiction to ours. The two systems cannot coexist. Wherever Islam gains a following, Muslims—that's right, individual Muslims—demand an end to human rights and the freedoms we take for granted. "Resist it while you still can," warned Christopher Hitchens, "and before the right to complain is taken away from you."

Clash Daily, July 25, 2017

Chapter 13: The Media

How the Media Elected Trump

Life is full of irony, and the recent presidential election is no exception. The irony is that, although they were in the tank for Hillary, the media were responsible for Trump's victory. Does that sound like a self-contradiction? Let me explain.

First, the media gave Trump an extraordinary amount of free airtime. The *New York Times* reported that Trump spent less on TV advertising—the single biggest expenditure for a campaign—than Bush, Rubio, Sanders, Clinton, Cruz, Christie, or Kasich. Bush spent 82 million. Clinton spent 30 million. Trump spent a paltry 10 million, but as of March 15, 2016, *he had received 2 billion dollars worth of free media attention.* That is more than the total for all the other candidates from both major parties.

"Donald Trump's campaign for president has received more nightly news attention than all the Democratic campaigns combined," reported *CNN*. "Donald Trump is everywhere," said *The Atlantic*. "The Republican nominee is all anyone can talk about. Whether this is because the media is doing its duty or because news organizations are capitalizing on Trump's bombast for ratings and traffic is a matter of debate." According to *The Tyndall Report*, Trump is "by far the most newsworthy storyline of campaign 2016, accounting for more than a quarter of all coverage" on the evening newscasts of CBS, NBC, and ABC.

The media have tried to explain away their outsized coverage of Trump by saying they were largely critical of him. This is supported by the right-wing *Media Research Center*, which found that 91 percent of Trump's airtime was negative and focused on personal controversies such as his treatment of women and release of his tax returns. He was vilified as a racist, a "misogynistic bully," and a liar.

My view is that it doesn't matter if Trump's coverage was positive or negative. I have always believed in the old saw that there is no such thing as bad publicity. Trump's victory proves it. A study from Harvard's *Kennedy School of Government* concluded that, in spite of media anti-Trump bias, most of the Trump media coverage actually was positive *in its impact on voters*. "Trump is arguably the first bona fide media-created presidential nominee," the study alleged. "Although he subsequently tapped a political nerve, journalists fueled his launch."

The second reason to conclude that the media was responsible for Trump's victory is that anti-Trump media bias drove many undecided voters into his camp. In other words, the media's negativity backfired. "The media's Trump bashing may wind up having the exact opposite of its intended effect," proclaimed a *Los Angeles Times* op-ed piece. "With Trump calling out media organizations for their bias, widespread slanted reporting is bound to reinforce this point—and to backfire." *Executive Intelligence Review* senior editor Jeff Steinberg said, "Media elites thought they were shaping public opinion, and they were, but in favor of Trump because anyone who the mainstream media hates is just fine with them." Writing in *American Thinker*, Karin McQuillan suggested that "the more the media attacks Trump as the second coming of Hitler, the more his supporters become determined to elect him and the more independents join our side."

Agreeing that media bias backfired, one voter wrote, "The bias was so obvious that it created sympathy (and votes) for Trump. People simply rebelled against a 'rigged' (media) system." Another voter said, "I can't sit idly by and allow these perpetrators of fraud to celebrate. Essentially, I am voting for Trump because of the people who don't want me to." Here is the reaction of one disaffected voter to anti-Trump bias on *NPR*:

> *"I slammed the radio off after getting so angry at the biased report and decided that moment I am voting for Trump. I had heard the bias before, always kind of subconsciously ignored it. This time I couldn't. I stopped listening to sound bytes from mainstream media, I started listening to full speeches of Trump. When I did that, the most obvious bias became apparent, and today NPR just blew the lid. This media bias is real, it's really intense and it pisses me off."*

"The media are in full panic mode because the American people rejected their leftist agenda—and them," said *Media Research Center*'s president Brent Bozell. Thanks to the election, media bias has been exposed for what it is. The mainstream media had better clean up their act or they will become nothing more than a bad joke.

Daily Surge, December 6, 2016

When Is Trump Going to the Toilet and Other Media Revelations

It is not difficult to understand why so many Americans have a negative opinion of Donald Trump. And that's not because Trump deserves a negative review. It is strictly thanks to our corrupt media.

The media sought to torpedo Trump before the election but they failed. Ignoring the opportunity to modify their slant in favor of objective reporting, they are instead ramping up the volume of malicious lies. "According to recent polls," says the *New York Times*, "the image of Donald Trump as a bigot has begun to crystallize, and for good reason: Because it's true!" A columnist writing in the *Washington Post* says, "Let's not mince words: Donald Trump is a bigot and a racist." Subtle. For those who still read this kind of yellow journalistic garbage, coming away with a positive view of President-elect Donald J. Trump is all but impossible.

The media also give inordinate space to the ravings of senile Democrats. They love to quote Harry Reid: Trump is a "sexual predator" who has "emboldened the forces of hate and bigotry in America," says Reid. "Winning the electoral college does not absolve Trump of the grave sins he committed against millions of Americans," argues Reid. Trump must "roll back the tide of hate he unleashed."

Let's not forget to include the avid reporting of good old Bernie Sanders' ignorant rant: "To the extent that [Trump] pursues racist, sexist, xenophobic and anti-environment policies," says Sanders, "we will vigorously oppose him." Smoke some more grass, Bernie.

The latest rash of lies centers around Trump's transition to the White House. Consider this *New York Times* headline: "Trump Transition Team in a State of Disarray." Disarray marked by firings and infighting, so it is reported. This blatant falsehood has been denied emphatically by the Trump team. According to both the *Times* and the *Washington Post*, Trump is wavering on immigration and wavering on his promise to repeal Obamacare. Both allegations repudiated by Trump himself.

Now let's set the record straight: *None of this spiteful reporting is true.* You can make an argument—albeit a misleading one—that many bigots have supported Trump. This does not make him a racist. But just as Hillary Clinton was guilty of virtually every evil misdeed she attributed to Trump, the media assault on Trump would be more aptly aimed at the Democrats. As pointed out by Rep. Mo Brooks (R-Ala): "It's a part of the Democratic Party's campaign strategy to divide Americans based on skin pigmentation and to try to collect the votes of everybody who is a non-white on the basis that whites are discriminatory and the reason you are where you are in the economic ladder is because of racism." Obama, Brooks says, is the most "racially divisive" president America has seen since slavery was abolished. Rest assured you won't read that in the *New York Times*.

The media attacks on Trump have reached a mad crescendo. According to NBC, not informing the media pool that he was going to dinner shows that Trump is guilty of a "lack of transparency." Commenting on the absurdity of this argument, Sean Hannity facetiously suggests that the media ought to be informed when Trump goes to the toilet and whether it is number one or number two, so they will know how long he will take. But here is the best one: Trump's decision to forgo his presidential salary is alleged to be in violation of the Constitution. Although it was okay for Herbert Hoover and John F. Kennedy, this decision, says *The Atlantic*, suggests that Trump "holds himself above the ordinary rules." With our biased media, you just can't win if your name is Donald Trump.

Daily Surge, November 16, 2016

A Lesson for the Biased Media

Throughout the presidential campaign, the Left and their media supporters floated the manufactured assertion that Donald Trump is racist, fascist, and misogynistic. Many weak-minded voters swallowed the Kool-Aid. Taking her cue from the press, a woman posted on *Facebook* that Trump is "a vile, orange, bloated, narcissistic, dangerously thin-skinned, spineless, lying miscreant." But this media strategy, initially designed to destroy Trump's appeal as a candidate, didn't work because there was an insufficient number of fools among the electorate. Now the same lie is being used by the Democrats, in conjunction with Rep. John Lewis' unsubstantiated claim that the Russians hacked the election, to explain away the failure of Hillary Clinton's candidacy. The assertion about Trump is, and has always been, completely false.

Enter MSNBC and its mouthpiece, Rachel Maddow, who a friend of mine refers to as "Rachel Madcow." She criticized Trump's acceptance speech on the grounds that it was "militant" and "anti-Semitic." Referring to Trump's "America First" slogan, Madcow said it has "very dark echoes in American history." She was alluding to the America First Committee of the 1930s that was infiltrated by Nazis. Terry Moran on ABC agreed that Trump's speech had anti-Semitic "overtones." *Meet the Press* moderator Chuck Todd called the speech "surprisingly divisive." Not to be outdone, Chris Matthews on MSNBC called the speech "Hitlerian!"

By aiming to unify the country in its own self-interest, Trump is being described as divisive and Hitlerian. Once again, I shake my head in disbelief that such nonsense is circulated by the mainstream media. Does Madcow really believe this crap or is she as deranged as she seems? Comparing Trump's slogan of America First to the isolationist position before World War II is a distortion of history. Trump wants to substitute love of country for Obama's anti-American ideology. How does this make Trump out to be anti-Semitic? Hitlerian? On what planet is there a logical connection? Not this one, to be sure.

If we are going to accuse anyone of anti-Semitism, let's stick with Obama. As Alan Dershowitz has finally figured out, Obama lied to the Jewish community from day one. "From lifting sanctions on Iran to calling for Israel to return to its indefensible 1967 borders," said the *Washington Times*, "Mr. Obama has spent the past seven years betraying America's treasured friend." Trump, in stark contrast, has expressed unqualified support for Israel. His daughter and grandchildren are Jewish. Nothing Hitlerian about that.

Nor can we call Trump's intention to place limits on Muslim immigration "Hitlerian." Trump has taken serious criticism because he understands the threat posed by Islamic terrorism and the unwillingness of Muslims to accept our values and assimilate into our communities. Obama's failure to mount a serious response to the 28,000 instances of Islamic terrorism since 9/11 is reprehensible. Hillary was hell bent on perpetuating Obama's head-in-the-sand policy. Let's be thankful that Trump is a realist.

Trump's acceptance speech was the first really positive, forward-looking expression of "American exceptionalism" that we have heard in a long time. He wants to "bind the wounds of division." He wants to give power back to the people. He wants to put an end to self-serving politicians who sell out their constituencies. He wants to put an end to Islamic terror. He wants to find "common ground" and "partnership" with the rest of the world. He wants safer neighborhoods, better schools, good jobs. To call him out as racist, fascist, misogynistic—and let's not forget Hitlerian—is insane.

If the media want to survive, they need to learn the lesson of this election. The mainstream media did everything in their power to elevate Hillary Clinton and destroy Donald Trump. They failed. We have proof that the public is not as gullible as it once was, that the propaganda disseminated by the press is recognized for what it is—not by everyone, but by enough voters and newspaper readers to make a difference.

Daily Surge, January 24, 2017

Part Five: Visions

"Put your future in good hands—your own."
Mark Victor Hansen

Chapter 14: What's in Store for America

Winning the New Civil War

The American Civil War of 1861-65 is considered the first "modern" war. Both sides used advances in communications and military technology that resulted in 600,000 deaths. Now, more than 150 years later, Americans are engaged in a new civil war.

This time it is not a war of armies and weapons and regional animosity—it is a war of visions. Liberals and conservatives each have a different vision for the future of the nation. Conservatives believe in the Constitution and the rule of law. The vision of "progressive" liberals is an authoritarian socialist nation run by unaccountable bureaucrats—an approximation of Venezuela, somewhere between Stalin's Soviet Union and Orwell's *1984*. The conflict over these value systems has escalated into the new civil war.

We have many strong indications that this is a hot war: the depredations of Antifa, a contemporary incarnation of Nazi brown shirts; Maxine Waters urging liberals to confront Trump supporters; mobs threatening the homes of prominent conservatives; the attacks on Justice Brett Kavanaugh; and the attempted impeachment of President Trump by partisan Democrats in the House.

The war began when Barack Obama was elected president. After promising just the opposite, the Obama presidency played into the leftist strategy of "divide and conquer." The fraud known as identity politics was a child of the Obama years. Using their perverted version of "diversity," the Democratic Party—under the leadership of Obama—exploited discontented elements in American society to foment division and hatred. Obama's comments in case after case—lies and distortions—stoked the fires of racial discord. After eight years of Obama, relations between conservatives and liberals were worse than ever and the country was plunged into darkness.

This new civil war is much more intimate than the old one. Instead of North pitted against South, we have friend against friend, neighbor against neighbor, brother against sister, wife against husband. It may be happening on your street or even in your bedroom. Try as you may, you cannot escape its tentacles. Author Mark Levin calls this phenomenon the "balkanization" of society. The Left's objective, Levin says, is to "collapse the existing society" by dividing the people against themselves. It appears to be succeeding.

The most alarming danger posed by the new civil war is the possibility that the United States could evolve into a totalitarian state within a few short years. Our system of government is strong because of "checks and balances." One such check is the existence of multiple political parties. Now try this on for size: A rogue political party seeks a take-over of the federal government by forcing the other party out, ending checks and balances. That happens in totalitarian states, you say, not in the good old US of A? Well think again, because that is exactly what the Democrats have been up to since Trump won the election in 2016.

If the current crop of Democratic Socialists can win back both houses of Congress and the presidency, their stated aim will be the imposition of socialism and the eradication of the two-party system. The Democrats have figured out that they can rule unchallenged by opening the border to millions of "refugees" who are expected to vote for Democratic candidates. "If we can't get enough Americans to vote Democratic, we will have to import them." Attempts to invalidate Trump's election are in service of this objective.

If you think I am simply an alarmist, remember that the Democrats have already succeeded in making the Republican Party irrelevant in California, New York, and Illinois. In those jurisdictions, Republican voters have effectively been disenfranchised. The Democrats are working overtime to do the same thing in Texas, Virginia, New Jersey, and other key states. If they had captured Texas in 2016, Hillary would be president—that's how close it is.

Keeping Trump in the Oval Office and winning back the House should be the primary objectives of anyone who cherishes individual rights over big government. The alternative is an authoritarian socialist nation run by an elite cadre of Democrats fronting for unaccountable government bureaucrats—the Deep State. Washington bureaucrats will be the ultimate winners if the civil war is lost. The antidote to a Deep State victory is Donald Trump. He is their Kryptonite and they know it. The Mueller investigation didn't work so now the Left is pushing impeachment to prevent a Trump landslide in 2020. My prediction: Trump will win in spite of all their efforts to defeat him. The war will be won by the Right at least until 2024.

Flag & Cross, November 17, 2019

The Two Biggest Threats Facing America

We are engaged in an ideological civil war for the future of America. The American Left and its senior partners, the Democratic Party and the mainstream media, are intent on destroying everything that is extraordinary about this country. Their methods—developed decades ago and refined during the Obama presidency—include the endorsement of socialism and open borders; a coordinated attack on free speech and other individual liberties; the ruthless indoctrination of our young people by left-leaning faculties at leading colleges and universities; an avalanche of fake news disseminated by a biased media; and the demonization of conservatives, whites, and especially white men.

The election of Donald Trump signaled a repudiation of the Left's platform. Trump's accomplishments are setting the train back on the tracks after eight years of Obama's subversive policies. It has not been easy. Obama's leftist supporters are doing everything possible to disenfranchise the 63 million Americans who voted for Trump. The Democrats are increasingly moving in the direction of outright folly with their advocacy of socialism, abolition of the rule of law, and the "Green New Deal." But if Trump is re-elected in 2020, as I expect he will, what do we have to worry about? The answer: the damage that can be done in 2024 and beyond.

The two most serious threats that we ought to be focused on now are: (1) Mass illegal immigration and (2) The brainwashing of college students. If unchecked, both will eventually lead to the destruction of the two-party system, the takedown of American institutions, and dismantling of the Constitution. Both threats relate to the same ominous prospect—that the left will achieve its anti-American objectives.

Illegal immigration poses an existential threat to the nation. Both parties in Congress have failed to acknowledge the threat, let alone deal with it. When millions of aliens are permitted to enter the U.S. illegally, and sanctuary cities and states can deliberately disregard federal statutes, the rule of law becomes a thing of the past and we no longer have a country. The economic costs of taking in 100 million or 300 million or more "refugees" would tear us apart. The social costs of deadly drugs, violent criminals, and terrorists constitute the worst public safety issue since World War II. But the most dangerous likely results of open borders are the destruction of the two-party system and the forced implementation of socialism by the left wing of the Democratic Party.

The Democrats know that if they can add enough voters from among the immigrant population, a Republican will never again be elected to office and the Dems can (a) re-write the Constitution and (b) muscle through their Green New Deal or some other totalitarian socialist nightmare. Obama's ideological heirs will have a free hand in fulfilling his promise to "fundamentally transform America." That scenario has already played out in California. Thanks to the invasion of illegal immigrants, the two-party system no longer exists in the state that elected Ronald Reagan to two terms as governor. Conservative voters in California have been disenfranchised. Let that sink in.

The plan of the Democratic Party is to use dubious forms of ID in order to give voting rights to people who are euphemistically referred to as "undocumented immigrants." If the intake of illegals continues at the current rate, what has already occurred in California will spread to the rest of the country. The

Democratic Party will be in a position to impose totalitarian rule on the United States.

The same result will be achieved if the current crop of college students is successfully brainwashed to accept the Left's platform. Only one viewpoint is permissible at today's colleges and universities, and that is the liberal viewpoint. In some schools, says Walter E. Williams, professor of economics at George Mason University, the faculty ratio of Democrats to Republicans can be as high as 20-1. When the overwhelming percentage of professors identifies as liberal, it follows that liberal ideas are considered politically correct and conservative viewpoints are ostracized.

"They don't want diversity of ideas," says Harvard professor Alan Dershowitz, "We're seeing a curtain of McCarthyism descend over many college campuses." By discouraging independent thought, our institutions of higher learning are training a generation of gullible adults who will be cannon fodder for the Democratic Party.

Is the brainwashing working? "Whatever students may go into college believing," says author Benjamin Wiker in *The Blaze*, "they come out liberals. That's why liberals truly, sincerely believe that the more education you get, the more liberal you'll be." Recent studies conclude that a majority of college students are in favor of limitations to free speech and have a favorable view of socialism. Gallup found that 69 percent of millennials say they would vote for a socialist presidential candidate. In *No Campus for White Men*, author Scott Greer warns that the kids marching today to shut down a conservative speaker on campus could very well be the senators, judges, and newspaper editors of tomorrow.

The hope that our young people will recover from the Left's indoctrination camps is a long shot. A great deal of responsibility must be placed on parents who allow their offspring to be the objects of intellectual abuse. These parents ought to be pulling their kids out of offending colleges and threatening to withhold financial contributions. Otherwise, if these brainwashed kids vote in a Democratic president in 2024, Trump will be the last Republican president and you and I can kiss our individual liberties goodbye.

So do we worry about Putin's aggressiveness, growing Chinese power, Iranian-sponsored terrorism, and North Korean nukes? Yes, but the real danger comes from open borders and liberal education. The good news is that we have more control over internal threats than external ones. The bad news is that either one of these internal threats can lead to the same disaster.

It would be comforting to think that an informed electorate will thwart the Left's subversive intentions. But when asked why American voters have lost their ability to see through obvious nonsense, economist Thomas Sowell replied, "That was before nonsense became a large part of the curriculum of our educational institutions." So much for the shape of things to come. It isn't pretty.

Reactionary Times, May 6, 2019

Impeach Congress Instead of the President

Let me say it clearly—I am all for impeachment. For two years, Democrats in Congress and the Deep State were confident that the Mueller Report would provide solid evidence for impeaching President Trump. The failure of the special counsel to find proof of criminal activity in the White House has shattered dreams of impeachment and let the air out of the avalanche of baseless invective that has been aimed at Mr. Trump. The ironic result of this pathetic attempt to sabotage the executive is the undoing of the legislative branch of the federal government. So yes, I am all for impeachment—of our ineffectual and unproductive members of Congress!

An article in the March 2019 issue of *The Atlantic* summarizes the insupportable reasons typically offered by the Left in support of its argument for impeaching Trump. The author, Yoni Applebaum, argues that Trump has not kept his promise to "preserve, protect, and defend the Constitution."

> *"Instead, he has mounted a concerted challenge to the separation of powers, to the rule of law, and to the civil liberties enshrined in our founding documents. He has purposefully inflamed America's divisions. He has set himself against the American idea, the principle that all of us—of every race, gender, and creed—are created equal."*

Are you as sick and tired as I am of hearing this false narrative? None of it can be supported with proof. In fact, the evidence for all of these accusations clearly points in one direction—at Barack Hussein Obama. It was Obama who ignored the separation of powers by doing an end run around Congress with his numerous executive orders. By refusing to enforce a variety of laws, Obama encouraged contempt for the rule of law. We are dealing with his failure right now as we debate the legality of sanctuary cities and Trump's attempt to enforce existing immigration law.

Obama did everything he could to expand the power of government at the expense of individual liberty. During Obama's presidency, the government tried to insinuate itself into every facet of our lives. "Every single one of [Obama's] initiatives," says *American Thinker*, was "directed at increasing government control in every area, with a corresponding decrease in individual liberty." His positions in case after case stoked the fires of racial discord and moved the country away from meritocracy to an arbitrary system of race-based tests for "social justice."

What infuriates me more than anything is when the Left accuses Trump of subverting American values. Trump cherishes the values that Obama held in contempt: respect for the rights of the individual; free speech; meritocracy; due process and the rule of law; equality of opportunity via free market competition; and the acceptance of personal responsibility.

In spite of the facts, we never heard demands for impeaching Obama. The only reason Democrats want to impeach Trump is— they are upset that Hillary lost. Donald Trump is not the problem. The problem—the one few people want to acknowledge—is on Capitol Hill, not the White House. When you listen to Nancy Pelosi, Bernie Sanders, Elizabeth Warren, Kamala Harris, and their over-the-top colleagues, it is clear that they have an obsession for taking the president down even if it means hiding behind a series of obvious falsehoods. Trump is a racist, he is sexist, he is bigoted, he is anti-Semitic and Islamophobic. Trump attempted to obstruct the Mueller investigation. He is a fascist. He is Hitler! All without proof, without a scintilla of evidence. This obsession has taken precedence over the job for which they were elected. If they put that energy to good use on the floor of Congress, no one would be talking impeachment.

"Congress is a national embarrassment," says the *New York Post*. "Beset by gridlock and petty partisanship, it struggles to do even the simplest tasks." Just look at Congress' inability to resolve two of our most urgent problems. Efforts to reach bipartisan agreement on healthcare have been derailed. The broken immigration system is being ignored—a statute ending catch and release is not even on the table. Sen. Amy Klobuchar says she wants to be president so she can fix immigration. That is the job of Congress—*her job*. Why don't Klobuchar and her colleagues do their job?

This is the most "do-nothing" Congress in my lifetime. The number of committee meetings to consider legislation is fewer than one-quarter of what it was 30 years ago. According to Sen. Ben Sasse, executive branch agencies (the Deep State) now make our laws, not Congress. The inference is that real political power resides with unelected officials rather than with our elected representatives. "That's why I left," said Tom Coburn, the Oklahoma Republican senator who resigned in 2014. "You couldn't do anything anymore."

Instead of getting their real work done, Congress has become "a weakened legislative branch in which debate is strictly curtailed, party leaders dictate the agenda, most elected representatives rarely get a say and government shutdowns are a regular threat because of chronic failures to agree on budgets," according to *The Washington Post*. Congress "functions more as a junior partner to the executive, or doesn't function at all when it comes to the country's pressing priorities." If this continues, said former Senate majority leader Tom Daschle, "they're going to evolve, or devolve, into irrelevancy very quickly."

According to *The American Conservative*, the federal government has less support than King George III at the time of the American Revolution. "Perhaps the greatest mystery of American politics in the 21st century is how Congress can have an approval rating that dips into the single digits while, on average, more than 90 percent of incumbents win re-election." If our representatives won't do their job, let's impeach them. If we can't impeach them, let's vote them out and bring in people who aren't afraid to solve problems.

Reactionary Times, June 17, 2019

Democrats Are Intent on Destroying America

My book, *Tyranny of the Minority: How the Left is Destroying America*, argues that the Democratic Party has rejected the values responsible for the success of our nation. Here are just a few traditional values the Dems would like to trash: freedom of speech; the primacy of individual rights over unlimited governmental power; due process and the rule of law; equality of opportunity via free market competition; the right to own property and determine how that property will be used; acceptance of personal responsibility. The Democratic Party insists that our cherished values are obsolete. Entertain no illusions—the election between Trump and a Democrat in 2020 will determine if the nation as we know it is to survive.

Efforts to destroy American values reached a crescendo with Barack Obama's campaign to "transform" the nation. The people who voted for his "hope and change" platform believed he would make our lives better. They were misled. Obama is guilty of the worst offense of any president: he lied to us. Obama hates America. From the outset, his intention was to destroy our country. Reflecting his contempt for the Constitution, Obama's government tried to insinuate itself into every aspect of our lives. This was not the kind of limited government envisioned by the Founding Fathers. It was closer to the dystopian vision of George Orwell's novel, *1984*. Obama's version of big government eventually would lead to oppressive control over the individual and the destruction of our standard of living.

"The socialist Left," wrote Steve Baldwin in *Western Journalism*, "believed the Obama era was the best opportunity ever to transform America to a socialist-based economy, and to eradicate our commitment to a Constitution designed to limit federal power." Instead, something wonderful happened. The American people repudiated Obama's anti-American agenda by electing Donald Trump. "Obama's legacy is in utter ruins," says Matt Margolis in *Trumping Obama*. "His executive pen was really a pencil and Trump was the eraser. The Obama era—once seen as transformative and consequential—will now be a mere footnote in history." Andrew Sullivan concurs, writing in *New York Magazine* that Trump "has effectively erased Barack Obama's two-term legacy."

Trump is the most successful president of my lifetime. In his first two years, he revived the economy, cut taxes, slashed unemployment, pulled us out of the Paris Accord, stood up to Chinese economic deceit, defended the border, eliminated the Obamacare penalty, rolled back hundreds of onerous Obama regulations, and placed two conservatives on the Supreme Court.

Despite his achievements, the news is full of attempts to cast Trump as a divisive racist who is unfit to sit in the Oval Office. No president has ever been handicapped by equivalent "resistance" from the Deep State—unelected, unaccountable government employees who are loyal to the Democratic Party. Thanks to their influence, the public was forced to endure two years of the Mueller investigation into alleged Trump/Russia collusion. In the end, we found out that the allegations against Trump were completely false and that the investigation was nothing more than an attempt to invalidate a bona fide presidential election.

Undaunted by their failure to unseat Trump with the special counsel, the Democrats continue to bombard us with lies and falsehoods. The latest manifestation is the felonious attempt to impeach Trump led by Nancy Pelosi and Adam Schiff. When asked what crime Trump has committed that would justify impeachment, the Democrats have no response. Pelosi has refused to conduct a vote on impeachment in the House as required by the Constitution and Schiff insists on holding hearings in secret. In other words, Democrats are making up their own rules in a manner reminiscent of a third-world dictatorship. Instead of defending the president, the Republicans are out to lunch. Fortunately, Trump is quite capable of defending himself.

As we approach the 2020 election, the Democratic Party has been taken over by the lunatic far Left: Schiff, Warren, Sanders, Harris, Nadler, Ocasio-Cortez, Omar, and company. The party's presidential line-up makes Obama look like a conservative. Their platform is the endorsement of socialism, generous giveaways, unfettered immigration, and contempt for the rule of law. Who will pay for all of it? The Democrats have no idea nor do they appear to care. All they care about is preventing Trump from doing his job.

How are they getting away with this? Why are the Democrats allowed to divide the country with their unfounded attacks on the president? Why do otherwise intelligent people tolerate the racist, sexist notion that women and minorities are oppressed by evil white males? When will the justice system do its job by going after the real culprits—Hillary Clinton, James Comey, Susan Rice, Eric Holder, and others from the Obama Administration who demonstrated total disdain for the Constitution and the rule of law? When will the mainstream media revert to telling the truth?

The Democrats and their surrogates—the media, academia, Hollywood—are committed to a winner-take-all battle for the future of America. Prior to Trump, conservatives were unwilling to say out loud that leftist policies are treacherous. The most significant thing Trump represents is a push-back by the Right against the destructive ideology of the Left. There is a danger in remaining silent while a cadre of harebrained Democratic liberals transforms America into an authoritarian socialist nation run by unaccountable bureaucrats.

Can we remain faithful to American values? Do we have the fortitude to defend the Constitution? Perhaps Aldous Huxley was correct when he predicted that, as our liberties are being taken away from us, we will be brainwashed to enjoy our servitude by a combination of propaganda and recreational drugs.

Reactionary Times, October 27, 2019

Acknowledgments

The author is indebted to the following people for their assistance, advice, and encouragement: A.J. Rice, David Stadille, Dr. Fredrick Berke, Don Zirlilight, Christopher Cayce, Dr. Robert Luthardt, Godfrey Daniel, Jeffrey Gitomer, Theo Androus, Hon. Joel Blumenfeld, and Fran Wolterding.

About the Author

Ed Brodow is a political commentator, negotiation expert, and best-selling author of eight books including *Tyranny of the Minority: How the Left is Destroying America* and *In Lies We Trust: How Politicians and the Media Are Deceiving the American Public.* A nationally recognized television personality, he has appeared on ABC National News, Fox News, PBS, Fortune Business Report, and Inside Edition. Ed is a frequent contributor to *Daily Caller, Newsmax, Townhall, American Thinker, Daily Surge, LifeZette, Clash Daily, Media Equalizer* and other on-line news magazines. As a highly respected negotiation expert, he has served as consultant to many of the world's most prominent organizations, including Microsoft, Goldman Sachs, McKinsey, Learjet, Siemens, Philips, Zurich Insurance, Starbucks, the IRS, and the Pentagon. As a keynote speaker, he has mesmerized audiences in Paris, Milan, Athens, Madrid, Warsaw, Frankfurt, Singapore, Bangkok, Tokyo, Nairobi, Sao Paulo, Bogota, Montreal, Washington, and New York. Ed is a former US Marine Corps officer, Fortune 500 sales executive, and Hollywood movie actor with starring roles opposite Jessica Lange, Ron Howard, and Christopher Reeve. If you want to book Ed for a speaking engagement or media appearance, email ed@brodow.com.

Printed in Great Britain
by Amazon

79930787R00150